MORE PROACTIVE SALES MANAGEMENT

More ProActive Sales Management

*Avoid the Mistakes Even Great Sales Managers Make—
and Get Extraordinary Results*

WILLIAM "SKIP" MILLER

AMERICAN MANAGEMENT ASSOCIATION
New York • Atlanta • Brussels • Chicago • Mexico City • San Francisco
Shanghai • Tokyo • Toronto • Washington, D.C.

Special discounts on bulk quantities of AMACOM books are
available to corporations, professional associations, and other
organizations. For details, contact Special Sales Department,
AMACOM, a division of American Management Association,
1601 Broadway, New York, NY 10019.
Tel.: 212-903-8316.   Fax: 212-903-8083.
E-mail: specialsls@amanet.org
Website: www.amacombooks.org/go/specialsales
To view all AMACOM titles go to: www.amacombooks.org

This publication is designed to provide accurate and authoritative
information in regard to the subject matter covered. It is sold with the
understanding that the publisher is not engaged in rendering legal,
accounting, or other professional service. If legal advice or other expert
assistance is required, the services of a competent professional person
should be sought.

Library of Congress Cataloging-in-Publication Data

Miller, William, 1955–
    More proactive sales management : avoid the mistakes even great sales managers
make—and get extraordinary results / William "Skip" Miller.
        p.   cm.
    Includes index.
    ISBN-13: 978-0-8144-1090-5
    ISBN-10: 0-8144-1090-1
    1. Sales management.   2. Selling.   I. Title.

    HF5438.4.M5425   2009
    658.8'1—dc22
                                                2008044717

Printing number

10 9 8 7 6 5 4 3 2 1

CONTENTS

PART 1

INTERNAL TEAM DECISIONS

v

PART 4

INFRASTRUCTURE DECISIONS

PART 5

SELF DECISIONS

PREFACE

A man of genius makes no mistakes. His errors
are volitional and are the portals of discovery.
—JAMES JOYCE (1882–1941)

Sales management is one of the most important and skillful professions in business today, and yet we still don't get it right. We spend years in sales, do it well, get promoted, and then realize that what we did to become great salespeople has nothing to do with being great sales managers.

So, if you overcame these issues, learned new skills, and became good at this management thing, congratulations. Now it's time to get even better at it.

How? Here is a book that tells you what not to do and how to avoid bad decisions—the stuff you wish you had never gotten into. This booked is based on lessons from hundreds of sales managers who modeled ideas, tried ideas, implemented ideas, and flopped!

Who's going to argue with that quote above from James Joyce? Mr. Joyce must have been a smart cookie. Here is another phrase—a mantra for the sales and sales management world.

> In sales, everyone agrees you end up learning more
> from your losses than your victories.

The lessons learned from your sales and sales-management mistakes are ones you remember, right? So, it's time to learn from other sales managers who have made some mistakes and want to pass them on to you. There are some big mistakes as well as some small ones that ended up having quite a big impact on these managers. There are mistakes you have probably made yourself, or are in the middle of making, or are about to make but you don't know it yet. Scary thought, eh?

This is not to say that just because something goes wrong you shouldn't keep trying. There are always those second-chance circumstances where you need to grit your teeth and just keep trying. But I'm not talking about mistakes of the tooth-gritting variety here.

What I am suggesting is that when it comes to big sales-management decisions—the really important ones, the ones that make or break the year—you may want to play the odds. Don't think that your situation is unique, because it's not. Speed kills, and the longer you delay a decision, whether it's a wrong decision or a right one, the more it will hurt you.

In this book we'll take a look at sales-management mistakes both big and little—the kinds of mistakes anyone can make. That way you can avoid making the same mistakes and, quite frankly, get better without having to fail so much yourself.

ACKNOWLEDGMENTS

A book like this comes straight from great people and sales managers: Jim, Dave, Mitch, John, Chad, Robert, Mark, Glenn, Andrew, Don, Keith, Irene, Tom, Jim, Colette, Barry, Steve, Dana, Glenn, Phillip, Dennis, Tim, Jewell, Kevin, Victoria, Dan, Julie, Brett, Doug, Mike, Don, Bert, Jim, and a host of others. Thanks for leading the charge as well as responding to the need for "mistakes." Your input and sharing were more than helpful in making this book come alive.

Stu Schmidt, you have given great insight into sales process and sales velocity. Thanks for the ideas and concepts.

AMACOM, you are a great group of people. Robert, welcome to the team . . . it was on time, right??? Thanks. Ellen, as always, it's great to fight with you, and you should know that you are usually right.

To my sister Nancy: We love you and miss you.

To my great wife, Susan, and son Kyle: You are great inspirations to all you touch.

Finally . . . twins, Alex and Brianna, the original and getting stronger every day . . . BAM . . . you just *gotta* have it.

INTRODUCTION

The mistakes. The errors, potholes, bad decisions, missteps, and the oops. They are all very real for the sales manager. In the sales world, there is very little place to hide when these "wrong decisions" are made. Most if not all decisions affect revenue, and because the sales function is responsible for generating revenue in a company, the effect of these decisions is readily apparent.

Bad decisions also affect expenses. It always costs you something to right a wrong. But it may not cost you money. Time, risk, and reputation are also expenses. And why is it that everyone suffers when sales management either takes too long to make a decision, makes what it knows is a wrong decision (but ignores it), or in the worse case, tries to justify and rationalize the decision?

In my dealings with thousands of sales managers, the question they usually ask when they think about the sales-management mistake pit is: "What should I watch out for? Please don't tell me what to do—I've got that down—tell me what to avoid."

Well, to all you sales managers, this book is about some of the best—and some of the worst—sales-management decisions ever made. It should allow you to make some decisions without the fear of second-guessing yourself.

"AM I NUTS? IS THIS THE RIGHT DECISION TO MAKE? WHAT ARE THE REAL AND HIDDEN CONSEQUENCES?"

If you are one of the many who have asked that question, read on.

Mistakes in sales-management decision making happen in five different areas:

1. *Internal Team Decisions.* These are the tactical decisions about the individuals on the sales team you manage. They're usually about coaching, counseling, motivating, hiring, and firing.

2. ***Upward Decisions.*** These are often strategic decisions that take your boss or senior management into consideration. In fact, your boss or another senior manager may ask for your opinion about something that affects the entire company when making an upward decision.

3. ***Sales Decisions.*** These are the day-to-day judgments you make with your salespeople or sales team when selling your product or service.

4. ***Infrastructure Decisions.*** These could be compensation, quota, contest, and/or territory-assignment decisions that affect the entire team.

5. ***Self Decisions.*** Here, you are the focus of the choices that are being made. These are career-enhancing decisions as well as career-limiting decisions.

With all these areas of decision making, what are the most common mistakes that keep some sales managers tripping over their own feet while others sprint toward the finish line ahead of everyone else?

It seems when a good decision is made, all is well in the world. The sales machine hums. Sales management receives much praise, and the next big thing (from a revenue and earnings standpoint) is just around the corner.

But make one bad decision and the earth stops spinning on its axis. The ramifications are far-reaching: Very quickly, the sales team and the rest of the company feel the impact of this bad decision. Worst of all, people's confidence in you and in your sales team is shattered. Not only do they question your decisions, but they look away when you're walking down the hall on your way to that fiscal-review meeting. Ouch! Would you suddenly feel all alone?

Progress is good, but taking two steps back for every one step forward is not actually making progress. But if you can learn from mistakes—yours or other people's—you have a great chance of success. After all, being a member of middle and senior management is a very demanding job, especially in sales. The tenure of a vice president of sales is usually less than four years. *Less than four years!* With all the changes that are happening in the business world at such an accelerated pace, we hear many sales managers crying out for help.

Changes in technology, go-to-market changes, distribution-model changes, compensation, rewards, hiring, territory, culture, competition, corrective action, online, and product-mix changes all happen at the speed of the Internet. You struggle to make one change and four more stack up right behind it. And of course all of your decisions must be "right."

Four years, eh?

That said, here are some of the most common decisions you face on a daily basis. And here is what other managers have done right, what they've done wrong, and what, in hindsight, they would have done differently.

Before we begin, an FYI: When I say *sales manager* in this book, I am referring to *all sales managers*, regardless of title—from first-line sales manager, sales director, and vice president of sales, to executive vice president of sales and marketing.

Oh, and one more thing: This book offers a few examples and ideas you may want to use on the job. Feel free to use what you want. If you prefer an electronic version of any of the examples or tools in this book, go to M3Learning.com and help yourself.

PART ONE

1

INTERNAL TEAM DECISIONS

"If I had my life to live over . . . I'd dare to
make more mistakes next time."
—NADINE STAIR

Coaching, counseling, motivation, and team building are the building blocks for the people side of your job. Ironically, you took the job to help others, and then you find yourself needing help and wondering:

"Why don't they do as I say?"

"Are they stupid?"

"How could he make a decision like that?"

"I give my children less instruction and
get better results."

Sound familiar? The next six chapters explain some of the team decisions sales managers have made that have given them pause, spun their heads around, and made them wish the weekend was a lot closer than it really was.

1

We Are a Prospecting Machine!

"Of course my salespeople prospect. That's what they are paid to do. At least that's what I tell everyone."

Reality is a hard state to deal with. Rationalization is so much easier. Even people who *aren't* in sales know it is the salespeople's job to go find customers. Who else? Marketing generates leads, customer service keeps the customers happy, shipping makes sure the customers get what they ordered, finance collects the money, and so on throughout the organization. It's up to the sales department to go find and close new business.

Sales management agrees. Sales management creates compensation plans, contests, and rewards for salespeople who go out and find new business. They have 33 motivational speeches on why their organizations have to go broader and deeper in current accounts, as well as take business away from the competition. They spend gobs of money on training their sales teams to get new business. Their companies are counting on sales to get *new* revenue streams from *new* customers. Someone needs to tell this to the salespeople, because:

Salespeople hate to prospect.

Take a look at the salesperson in Figure 1.1. She's friendly, has a great smile, and seems stress-free. She's having fun, right? Prospecting's cool—and everyone always calls back. Yeah, right. Let's get real. The fact is, salespeople would rather do anything than cold call—and they usually do.

Sales management doesn't want to alienate the sales team. It wants to empathize with them. After all, the managers were once in the same place; they too issued the same proclamations:

Figure 1-1

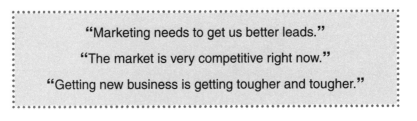

"Marketing needs to get us better leads."

"The market is very competitive right now."

"Getting new business is getting tougher and tougher."

Making these proclamations is a *huge* mistake. *Huge*. However, sales management has been known to listen to these voices and:

- Develop a prospecting-only sales department, also known as a lead-generation team. (This is different from a qualifying team, which works quite well for passive prospecting—leads that come into your organization.)

- Compensate salespeople *more* for generating new business.

- Actually believe that retaining business is harder than getting new business and designing rewards accordingly.

- Measure and reward for overall revenue and not break out new sales to new customers as an important company goal.

- Designate two groups of salespeople in the organization: Hunters and Farmers. Hunters hunt for new business, and Farmers maintain current business. (Great idea, until your competitor sets its Hunters against your Farmers. Then, of course, you have to deal with Trappers and Skinners—way too much classification.)

Sales management beware: Some of this organizational thinking may lead you to make decisions that will come back and haunt you.

THE FACTS

Progressive sales management in successful companies knows that customers churn.

> "How did my pipeline dry up?"
>
> "I thought my hunters were hunting."
>
> "When I looked at it, my salespeople were using less than 5 percent of their time proactively prospecting."
>
> "I asked my sales team, 'Who has asked for a reference in the past 60 days?' No one raised a hand, and the prospecting funnel is empty at the top for what reason?"

In addition, sales managers know that most customers do not buy all they can from one vendor, because they are not aware of the scope of the problems that exist in other departments within their own organizations. Opportunity abounds.

Calling high—that is, calling on people who are in upper management—with questions that let prospects think broad and wide within their organizations, and then creating a culture around this solid prospecting effort, takes sales management years to figure out. Let there be no mistake: The sales team that stops prospecting within its own customer base loses.

LEAD GENERATION VERSUS PROSPECTING

It is important to know the difference between lead generation and prospecting.

Lead generation is the act of targeting resources. It means figuring out where to hunt, what gun to hunt with, what to hunt, and when to hunt. Prospecting is the act of hunting. It means going through many fields and bushes to flush out the game, finding the game, taking aim, and pulling the trigger.

Prospecting = Hunting

A good lead-generation machine is no excuse for a lack of prospecting. Last time I checked, game doesn't just fall from the sky or knock on the door of the hunting lodge and say, "Here I am. Shoot me." The Internet has done a good job getting some game to knock on the door, but the really big game is still out there.

> *Prospecting Machine*: A company in which the sales department is doing well.

> *Nonprospecting Machine*: A company characterized by a weak sales forecast, a bad sales forecast, a weak pipeline, longer sales cycles, is closing bad business, or is closing deals based on price because the customer does not see value.

Sales teams, and especially individual salespeople, have the right to expect the company to do its part in lead generation. This could range from efforts to generate potential target markets and prospects, to qualifying teams (Q-teams) that qualify hundreds of leads, working them down to the most likely—the golden nuggets for salespeople to pursue. Great sales organizations have committed resources, up to 20 percent of their sales budgets, to lead generation, be it marketing dollars or sales dollars.

Taking the hunting analogy a bit further, you'll need to do some preparation before you grab your gun and head for the woods. Without putting together a strategy and culture around prospecting, you are looking at Mistake #1: Assuming that salespeople prospect, when they don't. Salespeople and sales teams need to generate leads. In fact, the sales team's focus on prospecting is the most measurable item of success or failure that I have seen inside of companies.

You get the point, right? The biggest mistake you can make is not to have a prospecting and lead-generation culture. The second biggest mistake is to have one but not measure it. You have to measure prospecting *even more than you measure revenue*.

● THE CURE ●

Sales management must do one or more of the five "its" to ensure an aggressive and effective prospecting culture exists.

1. Measure It

If you can't measure it, why do it? Your sales team is *not* above being measured on:

- The number of sales calls or qualified leads per week
- The number of executive prospecting calls or leads/month
- The number of prospecting attempts/connects/meetings per week/month
- The number of new deals per week/month/quarter
- The number of new deals in a current, installed, base account per month/quarter
- The number of new deals above $X per quarter

Sales managers who do not have a dashboard metric for prospecting are 20 to 30 percent less effective than the ones who are. This is a big number and should grab your attention.

Prospecting metrics need to be tailored to your individual situations. But the point is, measure it.

2. Reward It

The saying is true:

> **"It's rarely the size of the reward that is most important; it's the accolades and the praise that come with the reward that end up being of most value."**

How are you rewarding your sales team today? On what goals? Revenue and percent of quota to be sure, but what other rewards can you offer so the members of your sales team will feel good when they do something you want them to do?

- Do you have a gong or a bell people can ring when they close a new piece of business? (The Internet has gong e-mails.)   *Dо*
- Do you have your president personally acknowledge every new-customer deal? Do you have your president call the new customer's president or owner to thank that person for his or her business?   *Dо*

"Skip, you are so right. I was led to believe my people were too senior for basic metrics. When I implemented some prospecting metrics, they had a fit. All but one guy, who said he looked forward to beating the goal, which he did and has done every month. The rest of the team members, well, they copied my lazy behavior. I wasn't doing my job, which was to hold them accountable. So if I was not doing my job, why should I be expecting them to do theirs?

Bottom line, they complained, they threatened to quit, they went to my boss, which is laughable because what were they going to complain about—that they were being asked to find new business?

We measure the number of new presentations per month, the largest new deal per month, and the number of face-to-face meetings with vice presidents and above per month. They are called the Golden Three metrics. The reps know they are accountable for their quotas and their Golden Three. If they meet them, the revenue will follow, right?

What's really been cool is when a salesperson has a certain number of presentations to do per month and is trying to game the system by just doing some presentations to nonqualified prospects. The conversion rate— the rate of presentations to actual closes—as well as sales-cycle length for these individuals is much higher. Then as sales manager I have something I can do to proactively help.

What a mistake I was making by not measuring new business activity and high-level contacts. I believed the salespeople, and in reality, I was not doing my job. Never again."

- Can you start your weekly sales meetings off with a "New Business Report" or something that recognizes the people who have contributed?

- Do you have a "New Business Thermometer"? That's where the salespeople who have brought in new business during a month get their photos on the New Business board. The salesperson's picture gets placed at a higher level for every new customer the salesperson obtains. This is great for the salespeople who achieve and also for those whose pictures never leave the "Holding Area" (or whatever you want to call the bottom of the thermometer). It's better than a $50 check. Oh, and place the thermometer in the company cafeteria so everyone can see which people are doing their jobs, and which people are not.

3. Assign It

Suggestions do not work, and neither does hope.

Assign measurable objectives to each salesperson by week or month. You may be called a micromanager, but too bad. Salespeople will gravitate to the things they like to do or are the easiest to do, and they will avoid the "hard" things such as prospecting. Your goal is to help them be successful, and sticking their head in the mud (i.e., prospecting) needs to be an assigned measurable objective.

Your salespeople should provide some version of the following:

- Five new-name accounts per week

- Three sales presentations to new-name accounts, or three sales presentations to new departments in current accounts per week

- Ten proposals to new-name accounts per month

- Five meetings with VPs and above to new prospects per week

Assignments like these will create a culture where prospecting is a normal behavior, not the exception. Less than 10 percent of sales organizations assign prospecting goals; and as you know, you reap what you sow. Less than 10 percent of companies have prospecting goals, but they *all* have revenue goals (a reactive measure). If you want to win the game, you have to measure it one play at a time.

A great way to track these objectives is called the Skill-Improvement New Skills (SINS) chart (see Figure 1.2). SINS tracks assigned tasks for six weeks, until the salesperson feels that the assigned tasks are routine or a part of expected behavior. Then something else can be tracked with SINS. It's not like a negative productivity plan for a poor performer (most people on personnel-improvement programs, or PIPs, will be gone in a month); SINS is a cool thing. It could involve reading a book, taking a class, trying to develop a strong prospecting e-mail, learning how to leave an effective phone message, or actually trying to get to a certain C-level contact.

M²O/t in the chart means Mutually Agreed Measurable Objective over Time. The objective you want the salesperson to fulfill. Go read *ProActive Sales Management* if you want a detailed explanation of measurable objectives.

You use the SINS chart to make a salesperson a better prospecting machine as part of your culture, rather than being treated as an exception.

Date: _____

Skill-Improvement New Skills

Name: <u>Jim Smith</u>   Skill Set Focus: <u>Prospecting</u>

SINS

Goals	Strengths
M³O/t Week 1	M³O/t Week 2
M³O/t Week 3	M³O/t Week 4
M³O/t Week 5	M³O/t Week 6
Overall Assessment	Next Steps

M3
learning

Signed: Manager: _____ Salesperson: _____

Figure 1-2. The SINS chart.

4. Speak It

Every day! The more you talk about cold-calling, the success of getting new-name accounts, and/or additional new business at current accounts, the more attention the sales team will give it. Walk the talk. Get your butt out of the chair and go on some prospecting calls. Not customer visits, but cold calls. Go by yourself, don't just tag along with your reps. Go to a trade show and really work the booth. Keep prospecting front of mind. Make time for it. Use your contacts.

5. Enlist It

Get other departments and people to help.

Getting leads—especially good warm leads—is not easy. It takes a whole bunch of effort to find a prospect who is willing to talk to you, has a problem, has money to fund this new effort, and is willing to make a change. The more other co-workers or friends can help, the better, and rewarding leads is not a bad idea—but remember, the recognition is better than the reward itself.

Here are some things you can do.

- Go to other departments' staff meetings and enlist their help for leads.

- Have an Internet guru live in the sales organization to help capture home page hits, as well as what your competition is doing on its home page to generate leads.

- Go to lead-generation social breakfasts; have your salespeople go to them in the cities where they live.

- Go to trade shows at which your prospects exhibit, and get leads— and please do not say it won't work; way too many companies are successful at it.

- Find out how the customer service department passes leads, how it's rewarded for it, and how it's measured on it.

"I made the mistake of thinking that sales management did not have to be involved in prospecting. Business was getting a bit tight, and I needed to get something moving. I went out on a few prospecting calls with my sales team, and man were they bad. I wouldn't have let them back in again for a second call!

That experience led to all of us reviewing what it really takes for a prospect to be interested enough to call us back, answer our e-mails, or give us a second meeting. We now talk about prospecting every week. We all have enough sweat equity into how we are prospecting that no one on the team, including me, wants us to fail."

CONCLUSION

Sales managers have tough-enough jobs without taking on the added responsibility of empathizing with a salesperson over the lack of leads, how hard the market is today, and how they do not have the right product to break into the C suite. By far, the biggest sales-management mistake is lack of an effective, organized, and well-executed prospecting effort.

For the organization to succeed, a sales manager may have to do things that are unpopular but necessary. Getting the sales team to prospect—as a team and as individuals—and to do it well truly ends up making or breaking a sales organization. That's why it's the first thing in this book.

It's All About Luck

"I'm lucky to have Mary on the team.
She is such a top producer."
"Fred is lucky I'm his boss. With anyone else,
he would have been long gone."
"I'm a lucky manager to have such a great team."

It seems sales management relies on luck rather than increasing the skill sets of its players or recruiting new talent. For example:

- General Electric is legendary for turning the bottom 10 percent of its employees so the rest of the employees get better. Read any of Jack Welch's books for details.

- In sports, general managers and coaches are always tying to get one more top-notch player or are investing huge amounts in training facilities. They want their people to be better.

- Hotels are always divesting themselves of properties they do not need so they can acquire other things they really want—and make more money doing what they do best.

Luck? What is luck? If you want a great sales team, you have to plan for it, just the way everyone else does.

YOU MAKE YOUR OWN LUCK
BY RETOOLING

> "We don't rebuild at Ohio State. We retool."
> —JIM TRESSEL, HEAD FOOTBALL COACH,
> THE OHIO STATE UNIVERSITY

No, you do not have to divest yourself of salespeople or trade them to your competition for future draft picks, although the thought of that sometimes does seem pretty enticing.

The point is: Sales management makes a big mistake by reactively assigning territories and accounts to the teams it currently has rather than the teams it *needs* to have.

You as a sales manager have an obligation to figure out what skills your sales team will need to become competitive over the next six to twelve months. Train and educate your people so they have these skills. Test them. If they pass, they can sell. If they do not pass, they can leave, or they can go somewhere else in the company. They just can't be salespeople.

That may seem a little drastic, but consider these examples:

- A shipping department where the shipping people do not want to learn how to use FedEx online, costing the company hundreds of thousands of dollars

- An office administrator who does not want to learn Word or PowerPoint

- A salesperson not wanting to learn or use a customer relationship management (CRM) or sales-force analysis (SFA) system

There's a ton of new tools out there: CRM/SFA systems, Web-touch sales models, video selling, and other new concepts and ideas that sales managers are implementing. But what good are they if salespeople don't want to learn how to use them?

Take a simple test. Rate your sales team on one component: On average, how many words can your sales team type per minute?

Here are some interesting statistics.

Typing Skills for Recent College Graduates

- 1990: 15 words per minute
- 2000: 25 words per minute
- 2007: 55 words per minute

College graduates (for whom the ability to type a minimum of 40 words per minute is required to graduate from some schools) can type almost three times faster than graduates just 15 years ago could. Your average salesperson probably types less than 30 words per minute, and yet management wonders why salespeople don't readily accept and use technology.

Your salespeople are not lucky, and neither are you. Living in the future, defining what you need in six to twelve months, and actively acquiring talent and skills isn't luck; it's what the job is about! Here are three examples of how real-world sales managers tackled these challenges.

1. The sales VP who knew his sales team was going to be calling on people higher up in the typical organization chart trained his sales team on how to sell to the C suite.

2. The market was getting quite competitive, and margins were going down by three to eight points per year. The sales team took a negotiation course, and only the salespeople who passed the final exam with a 90 percent or better were allowed to sell to major accounts.

3. The manager of a worldwide sales team knew his organization was taking easy orders and not getting all it could or should because of a lack of communication among all of his worldwide offices. So he organized his major-accounts group into three teams made up of individuals around the world. He assigned ten companies to each team and then challenged the teams to beat the revenue and profit forecasts over a six-month timeframe on the deals they were closing. The game brought together the global sales organization, increased communications, and almost doubled orders from current customers. Almost 30 percent of the team that came in third was moved out of major accounts or quit within four months of the end of the contest.

IT'S NOT ABOUT WORKING HARD OR WORKING SMART

Luck, it seems, has nothing to do with the sales focus of the organization. The sales organization is about *selling*. The mistake many sales managers make is letting their organizations get off track and off focus. The conversations and meetings they have are about everything and nothing. Nothing to do with selling, that is.

Take this test. Get a piece of paper and write down the number 365 (days in a year). Then draw a line under that number and subtract all the days that your sales team is not selling. Figure 2.1 will show you how.

Now let's chart the results in Figure 2-2.

So where are you on the curve? Most companies are between 140 and 160 days (which means get your sales team focused; after all, selling for 150 days a year means your team is selling only three days a week). If you are below 120 days, you seriously need to get moving. And if you're above 180 days, well, perhaps you're miscalculating or not being realistic. Retake the test, this time with someone's help to make sure you have a fair assessment.

Days in a year	<u>365</u>
Weekends	−104
Travel time/month (typically 5–15 days)	−____ × 12 = ____
Sales meetings/month (typically 2–10 days)	−____ × 12 = ____
Other company meetings/month (typically 1–10 days)	−____ × 12 = ____
Lost days (weather, reorganizations, bad appointments)	−____ × 12 = ____
Vacations days (typically 10–25 days)	____
Holidays (typically 10–15 days)	____
Employee training (typically 5–10 days/year)	____
Employee territory review/month (coaching/counseling)	−____ × 12 = ____
Trade shows, company events/month	−____ × 12 = ____
Totals	Minus Days − ____
Subtract from 365	= ____

Figure 2-1. The sales selling test.

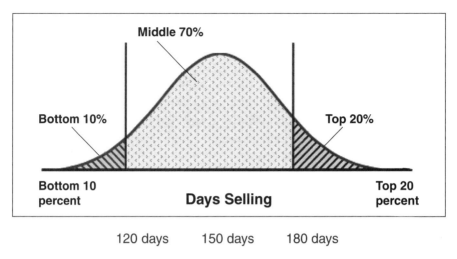

Figure 2-2. The sales productivity curve.

How can you get your sales team focused on selling? Adopt this simple, three-step method.

1. Change the Sales Meeting

2. Manage for Intradependence

3. Create the Reward System

Step 1: Change the Sales Meeting

How are your weekly sales meetings? Is everyone participating? Are the meetings too long? Do you not spend much time on customer issues? Here is a general rule: 70 percent of all sales-meeting topics are based on history. That is, they're about something that happened in the past—something you can't do anything about. So, keep your sales meetings on track by staying focused on current or future issues. It is your job as the manager to make sure all conversation stays in the present or future. This will keep your meetings focused and get rid of the bitch, moan, whine, and complain (BMWC) issues.

That said, sales meetings now should be no longer than 20 minutes . . .

period. Why would you want to take your sales team out of the territory for any longer than that? State the agenda, the issues, and the solutions; take questions; and you're done. The discussion must be about current and future issues only.

What about the quarterly sales meeting? Do the same thing, but focus on future customer issues. And the annual sales meeting should focus on selling skills and customer or market trends. Discussing product or company information should take no longer than half a day. Have the members of your sales team learn the product or service via e-learning—on their own time. You have more important things for them to do—like sell!

Step 2: Manage for Intradependence

Figure 2-3 shows how most managers manage for *dependence*.

This shows a typical span of control for a manager. He thinks that if he doesn't know what the organization is doing at all times, he can't be "in control."

This fear of loss goes to the *rewards in life are scarce* model (as opposed to the *rewards in life are abundant* model): Whatever information we get hold of, we need to hoard lest we be seen as not knowing, less powerful, and not in control of our own organizations.

Figure 2-3. Managing for dependence: the flow of information.

This model works well for the first-time manager who is learning the ropes—learning how to manage. It does not work well for a learn-and-grow organization and therefore should not be used after the first year or so of a manager's career. Figure 2-4 shows another way.

Figure 2-4. Managing for intradependence.

Here the manager has set the vision and the ground rules, and lets the team manage itself, with exceptions noted. This gives the manager the greatest span of control and allows him to live in the future—setting the goals for the team and letting the team work as a unit, then measuring the gap between goals and achievement—rather than get involved in every deal.

Intradependent managers manage to the top goals that need to be accomplished. The Critical Three (the CT) should help you manage in a forward manner.

Two Styles of Management

Kayte is a recently promoted sales director for a medium-size company. She has been in management for three years and is looking forward to her new job. She will have 4 sales managers and 26 salespeople working for her.

Karl has been in management for seven years and is in line for the vice president's job when it becomes available. He has been a regional director for two years, having been first a line-sales manager for five.

Karl makes his number every year. He is known for three things: working long hours, conducting monthly pipeline reviews (which are known as inquisitions), and cutting deals at the end of each quarter to make the quarter. He knows what each salesperson is doing on every deal. He gets 200 to 300 e-mails per day, owns two Blackberrys, and the reps know not to make a move without getting hold of Karl. Say what you want; it works.

The recently promoted Kayte does things a bit differently. She has her managers set weekly goals for their teams at the Monday-morning meeting. She reviews the quarterly "Crucial Three," the three things the team must accomplish for the quarter. She notes what each manager is doing to accomplish his or her Critical Three goal, and she redefines the metric every meeting. Additionally, she has the list of up-and-coming Critical Three to make sure her team can manage itself.

Two different management styles; both successful. One leverageable, one not. Guess where the A players want to work?

The Critical Three. It seems there are thousands of details that make up the decisions that fill a manager's day; too many details, too many fires, everything is important. The Critical Three (or CT) should go a long way toward keeping you and your team focused on what is important. They should be at your side and keep you focused on the day. Ask yourself two or three times a day if you are working on something that will move your CT. That will get your attention.

The CT is a weekly working document. Managers have their own CTs and the CTs of their direct reports. The CTs list the objectives for the direct reports. Figure 2-5 provides an example.

The Critical Three (CT)

The Goals for the Quarter:

1. Make the $8.0M quarterly revenue goal with a 1.4 forecast factor and 85 percent forecast accuracy on the 30-60-90 day forecast, with average sales-cycle length of 33 days.
2. Get 100 percent headcount filled and identify two bench candidates per manager for potential new/replacement hires.
3. Launch and have 20 percent penetration rate of new product by quarter end.

What objectives are being accomplished that contribute to the CT?

Manager #1
1.
2.
3.
4.
5.

Manager #2
1.
2.
3.
4.
5.

Manager #3
1.
2.
3.
4.
5.

What CT items are coming up?
1.
2.
3.

Figure 2-5. A sample Critical Three (CT).

The Rules of CT. There are four rules for the CT.

1. The number of objectives is not fixed. Although there are five listed on Figure 2-5 under each manager, two, three, or four works just as well.

2. The CT is not a taskmaster's list. You need to treat employees with respect and let them manage themselves.

3. Items can be added and subtracted only by mutual consent.

4. Everyone needs to reference the CT a few times every week. The CT represents the 80 of the 80/20 rule, and these items are what your managers or salespeople should think about daily.

Step 3: Create the Reward System

No, it's not just about compensation, it's about tasking your best salespeople with keeping the rest of the sales team on track. It's a sales *team*, right? Have the team measure itself on its sales focus rather than its BMWC focus. Reward for:

*   Best competitive win

*   Largest new deal in the month or quarter

*   Highest quantity of new deals in the month

*   Best forecast accuracy in the quarter

*   Highest number of calls to vice presidents in the week

*   Highest number of list-price deals

You get the idea. Reward things that *cause* results. If you are going to reward in the cause/effect paradigm, do not make the mistake and reward for effect (such as for getting the order). Instead, if you reward the *causes*, the effects will be greater than you anticipated. Sometimes it's your paradigms (or a salesperson's own paradigms) that are holding the salesperson back.

Tip. A quick word on compensation is in order. It is better to have one person in your employment making a lot of money than it is to have two people making an average amount of money. The mistake most sales managers make is to allow the B and C players to influence decisions and not fully support the A player.

It was a free-for-all. After the sales meeting, I counted eight contests: five from the product-line managers, two from marketing for selling certain combinations of products and services, and one from the president.

The members of the sales team knew if they sold something, they were going to get extra money. There was so much "free money" floating around that the salespeople did not really change their behavior for the rewards. They just collected the reward when they happened to sell something that had a bonus.

There was too much emphasis on effects and not enough on what the team needed to do. What a waste of company resources.

You have to pay for the best, but pay does not mean salary alone. Training classes, performance bonuses, and higher commissions on high-margin items all count. *If your choice is ten normally compensated salespeople or eight superstars, take the eight.* Keep the bar high, and always reset the bar. Remember, a sales-superstar's job is to do the impossible; a manager's is too.

Salespeople Are Self-Motivated

"What else can they ask for?"

You give them quotas, territories, good products and services to sell, competitive pricing, leads, and pretty good management. Heck, this stuff should sell itself. So what is it that makes good salespeople great? Is it their product knowledge, inner drive, motivation, luck, hard work, or organizational skills? Sure, there is a lot to these skills, but what separates the good from the great is the discipline of the sales team. Great salespeople have the discipline to:

- Prospect all the time
- Prospect at the right levels
- Qualify and disqualify prospects
- Use sales skills and learn new skills
- Use communication skills to get their message across
- Listen—*really listen*—to customer needs and what they want to buy
- Negotiate for a win-win outcome

The list could go on and on. These are common traits that all salespeople believe they possess or are working to improve. They think they have them or have enough of them to be successful. So what's the mistake they're making here? You.

LEAVE ME ALONE, GIVE ME WHAT I ASK FOR, AND I'LL MAKE THE NUMBER

It's a business, right? Salespeople will tell you they run their own businesses. They are in charge of their own destinies. They have their territory, their customers, their quotas, and their relationships. If they perform and make their numbers, just leave them alone.

Really?

In fact, when I asked managers to list mistakes they have made over their career, this was the second most common one they reported. It's not a battle over who has ownership of territory, customers, or quota. What is it then? It's the 20 percent gap.

> *The Law of the A Player:* A players take one year to learn, one year to master, then one year to get bored and look for something else to do.

Knowing this, managers do very little to keep the skill sets of their sales teams up to the level needed. Sales management is screaming for sales teams to sell value; at the same time, managers make salespeople sit through hours of product training. It doesn't work. What does work is a basic understanding of the 20 percent gap, which is represented in Figure 3-1.

During years one and two, which are marked by the letters A and B, the salesperson is motivated and successful—surpassing expectations and on the rise. At about year three, marked by C, everyone is telling the salesperson, especially a top performer, that he or she is doing really well. The salesperson, of course, believes it and begins to develop "success patterns."

A players have a certain presentation they are confident in. They make good contributions in those key meetings. They use specific marketing collateral; they have certain internal people they call on for customer-facing

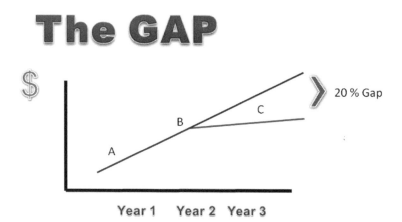

Figure 3-1. The 20 percent gap.

events. They know current accounts or territories well; they can always get a reference.

Whatever these patterns are, they were good enough to get the salesperson to her current level. But they're not necessarily the skills needed to keep this person motivated and going to the next level. The salesperson becomes complacent and really believes he is that good. The talent, drive, and questioning ability that got him to point B begins to diminish. There is no need to work as hard, because everyone is saying, "You really are *that* good."

A players have a book of business that needs to be maintained, so they focus on that. Oh, and by the way, they get new business too. But the energy that was working for the A player has dimmed a little. That's the 20 percent factor. Your A players could be using 20 percent more bandwidth than they're currently using.

What are you going to do about it? Here are some common responses from sales managers.

- "I'm not messing with success. John is an A player, and I have other problems."

- "Gail is doing great. She is at the top of her game."

- "If Jill can't do it, it can't be done."

There is nothing wrong with self-motivation and drive. Your top sales-people and top managers have it. What is lacking—and where you need to help—is coaching. In other words, you need to create the vision and set the goals.

Creating Vision

Telling the forest from the trees is hard, especially for someone who has been in the forest for so long. The primary job of the sales manager is to provide the vision, the direction, and the ideas for all employees, especially the top performers. But top performers have achieved success with their old patterns. So why change?

Top performers should change because those success patterns are not what got them to where they are today. It's not their current activities that mark their success, it's their ability to scope out the landscape, create a vision, get support for the vision, and implement it. That's what they did with their cus-tomers before they got so good; and through coaching, you can help them get back to those building blocks of success.

Setting Goals

Without goals (preferably short and long term—and written down), how do you know what success is? By measuring revenue? That's common enough, but why not aspire to a higher level of management and metrics? How? By measuring causal goals, not effects.

Goals should be reviewed monthly, and many should have nothing to do with revenue. They should be specific and should be somewhat hard to accom-plish. Remember, that's how your top performers became top performers. The goal sheet in Figure 3-2, which is similar to the Critical Three, is a great exam-ple of what you should be doing for all your employees on a monthly basis—es-pecially the A players. Remember, the idea is to be proactive, and revenue is a *reactive* measure. Simply put: Goal management is one of the most influential ways a manager can ensure success.

Creating vision and setting goals are two tools that can help you take your organization to the next level (which is what you are being paid to do). Without vision and goals, all you are doing is asking hamsters on treadmills to run faster each year. And as you know, after a while, the hamsters just can't run any faster.

The Goals and Vision

Vision for the quarter: To call higher and break into two new accounts at a senior-management level.

Goals:

1. Call on 5 new major accounts at the VP level or above for a 308-minute introduction meeting.
2. Develop and give a new value presentation that is at least 50 percent interactive.
3. Call 10 current VP customers and get a reference.

Progress on a monthly basis (or weekly)

Goal #1

1. _____
2. _____
3. _____
4. _____
5. _____

Goal #2

1. _____
2. _____
3. _____
4. _____
5. _____

Goal #3

1. _____
2. _____
3. _____
4. _____
5. _____

Figure 3-2. The Goals and Vision template.

—————• YOU HAVE TO KEEP SCORE •—————

Management, especially sales management, takes a lot of work. There is no need to list all the tasks and duties required, but as you know, there are a lot. So who is keeping score? Sure, revenue is the ultimate measure—the final score. But who is keeping track of all the statistics along the way? Consider what people in other professions would do.

- Imagine a professional football coach knowing only the score of the game and then having to figure out what strategy to use and plays to call.

- Imagine an actor who, with only a script in hand, is told to perform without knowing the other characters' parts or the plot of the play or movie.

- Imagine a tennis coach who only knows the score of each set and match and is told nothing about how each point was won or lost.

The list can go on and on. So why do so many sales managers believe that looking at revenue—reported on a quarterly or monthly basis—is the right way to keep score? I'll cover more on what metrics to keep in Mistake #10, but for now, make a mental note that you or someone on your staff needs to be the official scorekeeper of vision and goals.

—————• MOTIVATION MAGIC: THE FEARS •—————

For the manager who wants to get the sales team to break out of paradigms, a quick review of fears is in order.

Napoleon Hill, author of *The Law of Success* and *Think and Grow Rich*, among other books, says that people's fears hold them back from accomplishing great things. He has named these fears.

Fear of *poverty*—the biggest one

Fear of *criticism*—what other people say and think

Fear of *ill health*—always a reason for not doing something

Fear of *loss of love*—fear of being alone

Fear of *loss of liberty*—cannot do what you want to do

Fear of *old age*—life is passing you by . . . look forward, not backward

Fear of *death*—the unknown, and you will be frozen in taking risks

The best managers know these fears and work with their organizations to quiet them within each individual so their goals and visions can drive the organization past its current state.

The sum of these fears for sales types are:

- Fear of the unknown

- Fear of failure

Fear of the Unknown

This fear stops self-motivation in its tracks. For example, hiring managers will keep a C player around because they fear it will take forever to find a replacement—and even when they find one, they can't be sure what they'll end up with.

Salespeople are afraid that if they prospect, they'll get rejected. They fear putting their energy into a new prospect that won't succeed. That's just too big a risk. They're afraid to take a chance because they do not know what the outcome will be.

The fear of the unknown is easy for the manager to overcome. The key is to be aware of it, not simply to deliver corny motivational phrases, such as:

- "Sales is a numbers game. You just have to get out there."

- "Hey, every salesperson faces that. Here's what I did . . ."

- "You know, you just have to roll the dice sometimes . . ."

Not only do these canned phrases not help, they get salespeople in a panic because they believe that the boss really doesn't get it. To overcome the fear of the unknown, great managers ask great questions in a positive, forward manner: "Bob, if you did that, what would the best outcome be? What would be the worst outcome? If the worst happened, how fast could you recover? What would you have really lost? What can you potentially gain?"

Great managers ask great questions to overcome fears.

Fear of Failure

The fear of failure makes salespeople run as fast as they can from a new idea or from change. This fear is sneaky—people just don't come out and say they have a fear of failure. Comments you may hear include:

- "Why try? You know what's going to happen."
- "We tried that a few years ago and it just didn't work."
- "Heck, even Diane tried and she fell on her face. It just can't be done."
- "Now that's stupid. Who thought of this one?"
- "I know it can't be done. Why try? What's the point?"

This fear surfaces in questions and emotions. Fearing failure, the salesperson or manager knocks the idea or suggestion. It's not that they won't try something other than what they are doing currently. There are two reasons they don't want to get on board:

1. *They have incomplete information (or so they think).* So instead of calling attention to something they don't have—information or the ability to get it—they attack the idea or suggestion by saying, "Here is why that won't work . . ."

2. *They lack perspective.* Without the desire and ability to see all sides, this fear will take over and blind the decision maker. He or she will say something such as, "I know that won't work. I tried that exact thing before . . ."

It is the proactive manager's job to overcome these fears when trying to motivate the sales team. Forget about the canned phrases. Ask questions, have team members uncover fears, and go forward.

───────● **THE SHORTER THE BETTER** ●───────

When setting goals and visions, remember: The shorter the better. Long-range goals and dreams are great, but the manager who wants to keep a team on track knows to measure goals in weeks or months. Visions should be quarterly. Goals should be an accumulation of timely events. The goal formula looks like this:

- *Gather* critical information on a *weekly* basis.

- *Adjust* the tactics you are using on a *monthly* basis.

- *Reward*, both positively and negatively, on a *quarterly* basis.

Figure 3-3 illustrates this idea.

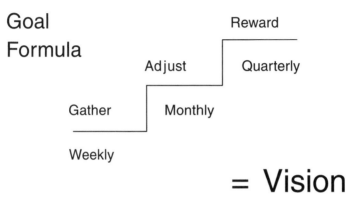

Figure 3-3. The goal formula.

SALESPEOPLE AND THEIR PARADIGMS

You have a new title: Paradigm Buster. What good are paradigms anyway? All they do is hold you and your team back. Experience?

> "Experience is what you get when you didn't get what you really wanted."

You need to help your salespeople break through their gaps, their fears, and their experiences—their paradigms. Please remember: What is good enough to get you where you are today is not good enough to get you where you need to go.

SALESPEOPLE ARE MOTIVATED BY MONEY

While I am on the subject of motivation, I need to debunk the myth that salespeople are motivated by money. Salespeople are not motivated by money. They are motivated by what money will do for them, not the money itself.

SALESPEOPLE ARE NOT MOTIVATED BY MONEY

Remember, the law of the A player states that in year three A players want more challenge to stay at their peak-performance level. Give it to them, and stop thinking money will motivate by itself.

Most companies are throwing money around as though it were free. In fact, it's called "Free Money" when a salesperson wins a spiff for selling something, but the spiff in no way helped the sale. The person thinks, "I have no idea why I am getting this $1,000 bonus check. I think there was a bonus on product A. Hey, no complaints here, I'll cash the check."

FINALLY

Salespeople are not self-motivated, not even the top performers. They need new goals, metrics, and challenges, just like you. Do your job and manage all your salespeople, not just the "ones who need it."

I'll Focus on My B and C Players and Make Them Better

"If I focus on the B and C players, they have a better chance of success. After all, these are the people who need my help the most."

This is a top-five mistake. Managers want to help, and they flock to the people who need the most help . . . well, who are the easiest to help. Hey, you feel good when you can help—and it's easy to help B or C players. They ask questions like:

> "What's 1 + 2?"

The top performers ask questions like

> "What's the square root of 2,751?"

33

You are ready to answer the easy questions; you have answered them your entire career. Heck, everyone knows 1+2 = 3. Time to bring out the flash cards.

Now, the square root of 2,751? Wow, that's a tough one. Where's that calculator? Maybe you should just answer the 1+2 question and move on to 1+3 and even 1+4 in a bit.

Top performers demand that you be at the top of your game and that you're not just regurgitating what you already know, what you have told others, or what you personally did years ago. It's time to get your A players to A+ status. That is where you should spend your time.

B AND C PLAYERS WANT TO PERFORM LIKE A PLAYERS

Now here is an interesting idea. Your B and C players want to perform like A players—they just don't know how. So guess who is holding them back?

The managers I interviewed claimed one of their biggest mistakes was treating subpar performers in a subpar way. For example, the manager who thinks he has a junior sales team will have the sales team acting and performing in junior ways. The manager who lowers expectations for the salesperson who has had a rough time, has a lousy territory, is a rookie, is a person who has not taken to the training well, etc., actually increases this person's chances of failure. Sound familiar?

The secret is for the manager to set measurable objectives that are equal for everybody and then manage the exceptions. When the A players exceed the expectations, drive them higher to new paradigms. When the C and B players barely meet or come just short of their goals, ask them what actions they will take to meet their goals. Usually, it's their failure to complete the activities to which they committed initially that cause them to fall short of their goals.

THERE IS NO SUCH THING AS B: ABILITY AND DRIVE

Along these lines, the mistake managers make with their B players is trying to help them. That's right: Help is usually not a good thing. By "teeing it up"

Minimum Playing Requirements (MPRs)

In Pop Warner football programs for kids ages 8 to 16, each team usually carries more than the starters. Some kids get a lot of playing time, some kids get some playing time, and some get very little.

Pop Warner's designation for these kids is MPR: minimum playing requirements. Each kid on a team has to play a certain number of plays each game, usually six or seven.

Well, you'll never guess what the coaches' expectations are for the MPR kids. You guessed it: the minimum. And guess who knows it. The kids.

So a championship Pop Warner coach calls his kids animals. The starters are lions, the second team is called the bears, the kickoff team is labeled tigers, and the goal-line defense team is known as the wolves. Each kid knows what animal he is, and the kids get to wear patches that signify their animals.

The parents of course got into it, and pictures of animals started showing up at games. Johnny's a wolf—Go Wolves.

These coaches did not treat the kids like MPRs, and as a result, the kids did not play like MPRs. Makes you wonder how sales management and their paradigms can hold salespeople back.

---

for the B player, all you are doing is encouraging dependency and weakness. You need to focus your managerial energies on ability and drive.

As a manager, how can you increase someone's ability to do something? How can you stimulate that person's drive?

People can gain ability through training. Great sales organizations require 40+ hours per year of classroom activities—skills training—for their salespeople and sales managers. These activities are designed to teach many types of skills:

- Selling skills
- Mentoring skills
- Qualifying skills
- Coaching skills
- Hiring skills
- Telephone skills

- E-mail-writing skills
- Corrective-action skills
- General business skills
- Presentation skills
- Negotiation skills
- Leadership skills

The list goes on and on. We recommend a team report card that describes what each employee has accomplished, what each employee needs to do, and how that employee plans to do it. This is not necessarily a formal human resources document, just a report card with a plan for improvement.

Drive is a different topic. Understanding what motivates your people and how you can positively influence that drive is a topic for Mistake #5. Needless to say, your ability to influence your B and C players' ability and drive are the key variables. The report card will help.

A IS THE UPSIDE

Here is a quick reminder. Say you have 10 salespeople, and each has a $1,000,000 annual quota. Typically, the distribution is something like what's in Figure 4-1.

Salesperson	Quota	Projected Actual
Bob	$1,000,000	$1,200,000
Mary	$1,000,000	$1,000,000
Jim	$1,000,000	$900,000
Dennis	$1,000,000	$900,000
Randy	$1,000,000	$800,000
Michelle	$1,000,000	$800,000
Alice	$1,000,000	$700,000
Fred	$1,000,000	$550,000

Figure 4-1. The typical sales distribution.

Logic says if you focus on the bottom players, you may get an increase in revenue. Heck, look how far off they are from their quotas! In reality, the opposite is true. If you focus on the bottom four, you probably can get an extra $300,000. But if you focus on the top four, you probably can get an extra $1,000,000. If you are looking for upside, go after your A players.   ←

C PLAYERS: TRAIN, SWITCH, DITCH, OR BITCH (TSDB)

When I polled top, seasoned sales managers about their below-average performers, they told me,

> **"I wish I would have made a decision on my C players sooner."**

But that's the wrong statement! They should have said,

> **"I wish my C players would have made a decision for themselves sooner."**

Your job is not to fire, reprimand, or TSDB these folks. Your job is to put them in a situation—their job—and measure objectives, note gaps, and have *them* make a decision about what to do. They have to close the performance gap, not you. Figure 4-2 illustrates that performance gap.

Your job is to document performance gaps, note the delta, and have the salesperson or sales manager list what she is going to do, what measurable objectives he is going to accomplish, and when. This is not the time to have the employee state:

"I'll do better."

"I'll get it done."

"We just have to work harder." (Note the *we* here.)

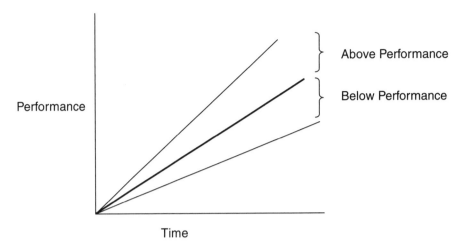

Figure 4-2. The performance gap.

Then you, the manager, end up with an albatross around your neck, and you have to take action. This clearly is a mistake.

True Story—"I Did What You Said."

"I reached out to my top performer, who was doing $250,000/quarter. His best quarter in the past few years was $350,000.

I asked him what would his best be in the next quarter, and he told me $300,000. That would mean $15,000 in commission to him. I told him if he could hit $600,000 for the quarter, I would pay him additional commission of course, but also we would lease him a Porsche for one year.

Because he is a car nut, this got his attention. He asked a few days later what it would take for us to buy the car for him. After much deliberation, we settled on $1,000,000 for the quarter.

Results: $607,000 and the car for a year. Is this going to set a new bar for the sales team for the rest of the year or what? Thanks again."

A great phrase you should learn to master is:

> **"What specifically do you plan to do, and by what date, to live up to your good intentions?"**

Is this a great phrase or what? When you get to Mistake #10, about metrics, you'll find the exact metrics you need to measure for this situation.

One more thing to note: An A player not trying to get to A+ status is in the same boat as the C player trying to get to a B. Your goal as a manager is to get your A players to A+ status. The gap concept can be applied to all employees.

● YESTERDAY IS NOT LIKE TOMORROW ●

In my research, managers mentioned that their ability and bandwidth to keep implementing change has diminished. Consensus management has stalled many initiatives, and decision risks have increased with the speed of communications. Tomorrow's sales managers will need to be faster with the things they can control.

Metrics at the individual level are items managers can control, so the need for gap metrics has increased exponentially. Almost all the managers I spoke with described the need to go to quarterly and monthly metrics. They admitted the first time through was clumsy, but not implementing it at all was way beyond the risk they were willing to take. The bottom line is to be proactive and set metrics that are much shorter in duration than ever before. Like the battleship, the annual review is dead.

Salespeople Are Motivated by Money

"By paying monetary rewards, in some cases large amounts,
and focusing these rewards on accomplishments,
the manager is motivating the sales team. Really?"

●————— MONEY: THE WINNER ●—————

It's the ultimate measure, the final check in the box. Yes, money can be used as a motivator. However, if you want long-term results, then motivate the members of your sales team with things that help them get money. And do it with an eye on changing behavior, not making them dependent on gimmicks.

Motivator	Short-Term Result	Long-Term Result
Money	Achieve Goal	More Money Needed
ProActive Metrics	Achieve Goal ——→	Behavior Changed

In the short term, money can get someone's attention, and salespeople will do whatever it takes to get the money that is offered to them. Somehow, some way, they will make it happen so they can get their checks. Usual contests that managers employ focus on results, not on behaviors. Contests that are money-motivated include:

- Spiff on a product

- Bonus for sales at the end of a quarter or month

- Extra commission for selling a product or a service from a partner

- Selling more product than the customer really wants to buy or needs

But contests that are ProActive in nature include extra rewards for:

- Sales to a new customer.

- Presentations to senior-level executives.

- Executive-homework sales calls, where the goal is to find out what the goals of the prospect are and not push your goods and services.

- Getting the most VP-and-above contacts via referrals from current customers.

- Any good, measurable prospecting actions.

- Anything that creates leverage. (Let's say you reward for the number of new sales calls per month at the VP level or higher. The salesperson will always find a sale, but now look at the other prospects he is calling for the first time. When the prospecting window opens, he already has a contact.)

If you are going to use money or some derivative thereof, make sure you target the rewards to ProActive metrics rather than give away free money to salespeople who are just doing their jobs. Focus on the behavior you want changed, not just a short-term hit in the monthly revenue forecast. From time to time, you may need to use those short-term hits—and that's okay. Just make being ProActive part of your strategy.

TOP THREE MOTIVATORS

When it comes to really motivating a sales team, you have to strike where the salesperson wants to get hit. It's a pretty simple thought process. What really motivates a sales team or sales individual?

#3: Money

As we said before, this seems to be the ultimate reward. Usually, sales management can throw a few bucks at a problem and have an answer for senior management, a proclamation that it is working on a solution to a problem. This explains the need for the contest.

For example, a manager might say: "We really have to get business jump-started to make the year. I am going to recommend we pay an additional 2 percent commission for the rest of the quarter. That will get the team fired up."

Do you know how silly this is? It's like saying, "Accounts receivable are now at 34 days outstanding. I propose we pay an extra 2 percent to the A/R team to collect the money more quickly." Or, "We are running a bit behind on shipping. We need to incentivize these shipping clerks or they are just not going to be motivated to ship out our stuff. Anybody have any good ideas?"

Here is a good idea: Have the shipping clerks and the A/R team *do their jobs*! "Sure," you say. "But in sales, of course, it's a different problem."

No it's not! Don't pay money for results. Money is not a motivator in the naked sense; it's what money will do for that individual that is the motivator. It will let a person buy something she always wanted to have; it will give her status among her friends and peers; it will give him a sense of security, and on and on. Use what money will *do* for the salesperson as a motivator. Don't just toss free money around.

#2: Praise/Reward/Recognition

Now, here is a motivation area from which you can really get results.

Who doesn't want a pat on the head, a thank-you for doing a job well, or acknowledgment from peers, management, and friends? Most salespeople are striving for this recognition, and management tosses this important motivator around like an old sock.

Ad hoc planning and execution in this area will get you ad hoc rewards. You need an annual plan for this motivator to be of significance. This reward plan comes in three sizes: small, medium, and large.

Small. Plan three small rewards for the year. These rewards are very loose and can be given out at a moment's notice. Examples include:

- Thank-you notes
- Thank-you e-mails
- "Gotcha" notes for catching someone doing something right
- Upgraded business cards for sales reps making their quotas
- A phone call from the president or owner every month to the salespeople who exceeded their quotas
- Remembering to say thank you to three people every day

Though small, rewards like these are very effective and very beneficial for salespeople, and they require very little work from the manager. Without a game plan, however, they will be lost in the day-to-day grind. You have to work at being effective, and these small rewards should be posted on your office wall. Figure 5-1 provides a template for this. *Do*

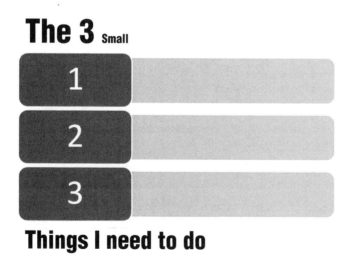

Figure 5-1. The small-rewards chart.

Medium. Medium rewards are for special effort, and you should base them on ProActive achievement. It's okay to give rewards to the top salesperson of the month, the year-to-date leader, and the person who made the largest sale in the quarter. Other specific achievements that might earn medium ProActive rewards include:

- Most cold calls for the month
- Most referrals
- Shortest sales of the quarter
- Most sales made without a demonstration

These rewards should not be cash. Cash has a way of being a very short-term reward, which is another way of saying that salespeople forget about cash quickly. They do remember:

- Front-row tickets to a sporting event
- A round of golf on a weekday
- A gift certificate from Tiffany & Co.
- Front-row concert seats
- A weekend vacation at a local resort
- Movie passes
- A Mont Blanc pen
- An Apple iTouch
- A portable GPS system

The list is endless. You can have a contest once a month based on what you want people to accomplish.

Large. Large rewards can cover the complete range—a watch, or a gold coin, or a year-long lease on a Ferrari. These large awards should be once a year—twice a year at the maximum—and should be based on results of the goals and metrics you established, not just top revenue.

A salesperson-of-the-year award is a great idea as long as you use more than just revenue as a deciding factor in who gets the reward. Large rewards are about recognition, not necessarily the size of the reward. Make sure there is enough praise and acknowledgment associated with the reward, or you will have spent a bunch of money for very little mileage.

One manager told me he won the Salesperson of the Year award in a company that had 200 salespeople. At the end of the year, the sales meeting was cancelled because of budget reasons—and his accomplishment went unrecognized. The next month, he noticed a $1,000 bonus payment in his commission check. Okay, he remembers this, but not in the most positive, rewarding sense. Recognition by peers is important too.

#1: Learning, Growth, Challenge

The number-one motivator by far in my research is the opportunity to learn and grow. Salespeople love challenge. They thrive on it. They also want to be rewarded by conquering new opportunities with no added risk, of course. Give them something they can learn or grow into and they will rise to the challenge. Examples include:

- Promotions
- A high-level training class
- Status as a new-product champion
- Executive sponsorship
- A temporary overseas position
- A position as a mentor to new hires
- A three- to six-month internal position with the marketing or contracts department
- Permission to run staff meetings in your absence

You can think of hundreds of examples; just beware the status quo.

The status quo is where you believe the salesperson is so valuable, there is no way he or she can be replaced, and therefore, this person cannot be given any of these learn-and-grow opportunities. By adopting this attitude, you are holding back your A players. And without this opportunity to learn and grow, they will:

> Get stale
> _____
> Get out

Neither of these options is acceptable, so avoid the status quo and start implementing some of these rewards.

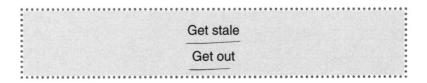

MOTIVATE BEHAVIOR, NOT RESULTS

You want to be a ProActive manager, right? At all levels of sales management, you need to look at what you are doing to effect results. If you are managing for revenue only, you are measuring against the wrong thing. Your job is to be ProActive. That's why you are in sales.

The Combo

I ran across a company while I was doing a sales kickoff speech where about half of the salespeople in the crowd were wearing letterman jackets. I'm talking about those jackets school athletes wear with the big letter on them that signified the school.

Well, it made me really want to smile and shake my head a bit.

I was in the process of smiling and shaking hands when the VP of sales came over to me and explained.

"When salespeople make their first annual quotas, they get a jacket. After that, they get merit badges for outstanding success in certain areas, like prospecting, closing new business, attending certain training classes, or learning how to do an ROI analysis. Each salesperson can actually get three or four badges each year. Some even have second- and third-degree badges, like Marie over there, who has a third-degree prospecting badge she just won this year."

"We kind of like combining rewards with learning and growing, and our jackets are a result of this thinking, and the reps love it."

Okay, they wouldn't give me a jacket when I sheepishly asked for one, but the results the company was getting from this combination motivation effort were outstanding.

If you want to stay in sales management and be great at it, then concentrate on behaviors, not on results. Behaviors will result in performance differences that can be measured, both positively and negatively. As a manager, you can preach all you want about the importance of reaching the final goal, but if your sales team does not know how to get there, then what good are all your motivational speeches? Focus on the behaviors you want increased, as well as behaviors you wanted decreased, by team and by individual. Only then will your results change over time.

M I S T A K E

I Am the Team Leader

"Sales managers don't really know their roles,
so they do the salesperson's job."

Ah, the good life.

How great is it to have so many friends? They love you. They adore you. They agree with you and they listen to you. They travel halfway around the world to see you. Popularity is your middle name. People want to play golf with you or at least have lunch with you. You, of course, also want to have them around as well. Well, time to get over that one.

STILL ONE OF THE TEAM

Being a member of the team can be the source of multiple mistakes.

- It clouds your vision.

- It tempts you to allow C players to hang on too long.

- It tempts you to allow A players to get soft.

- It stops you from doing your job.

- It forces you to focus on today, rather than tomorrow.

Time to define the role of sales manager. You know what it is not, so by defining what it *should* look like will give you a chance to model the correct behavior.

THE LEADER OF THE TEAM AND CHIEF DEAL MAKER (CDM)

That's what most sales managers believe themselves to be: chief deal makers (see Figure 6-1). Sure, there is a time and a place for sales management to get involved in a deal, but most managers I hear from tell me they are being dragged into the here and now far too often. Why do they allow themselves to get dragged down into this hole? Turns out their top reason is that they like the art of the deal. They have a tough time getting out of it because they really don't want to get out of it. Confused?

Figure 6-1 The chief deal maker.

LIVE IN THE FUTURE

Figure 6-2 is your daily to-do list. Copy this down. Monthly and weekly planners really don't work too well, because sales managers tend to want to accomplish goals and tasks *right now*.

Did you notice the lack of gaps in the schedule? Those gaps quickly fill with day-to-day things. It's all about delegation at this level.

Your sales process must include outstanding middle managers. If you are a first-line sales manager, you need a few great A players who have the required characteristics so you can be a great manager. If you are a second- or third-line manager, you have to delegate the execution of the current quarter. This includes discounts and terms. Now, there are some legal issues you may have to handle, but the managers I hear from are screaming that they need to get out of the day-to-day to do their jobs.

The managers who have accomplished this seem to work in the medium and long term—and they have become very successful at it. Finding future tasks to stay focused on is a top priority to avoid the mistake of getting dragged down in the day-to-day.

Sales Management Daily To-Do List

8:00–9:00	Senior staff meetings (this would be meetings with your peers or bosses)
9:00–10:00	Review/modify next quarter plan
10:00–11:00	Metric check (check on forecast metrics)
11:00–12:00	Free time (check e-mail, catch up with admin)
12:00–1:00	Lunch with someone outside of the company (customers, peers, consultants)
1:00–2:00	Review/modify rolling 12-month plan
2:00–3:00	A-player meetings to determine trends
3:00–4:00	Senior staff meetings
4:00–5:00	Day-to-day issues that could not be solved
5:00–6:00	Modify processes to make sure 4:00 meetings are as short as possible
6:00	Home

Figure 6-2. The daily to-do list.

PLAN FOR THE GAP

If you really want something to do, plan for the gaps. Welcome to Gap Charts (see Figure 6-3). These are going to rule your life from now on.

Note the A, B, C, and D points.

A—The starting point for your task/plan/objective

B—The stated goal

C—Early detection of above-plan variance

D—Early detection of below-plan variance

In simple math terms, determining early detection of plan variance is a given. It is why mathematicians get paid. Their job is to track norms and understand deviations. Imagine NASA launching a rocket and figuring out when the space capsule is halfway to the moon that it's 50 percent off course. You want to catch that error as early as possible, right? Same with sales management. It's time to create and track norms. Figure 6-4 is a sample you can use.

Figure 6-5 shows the Gap Chart in action.

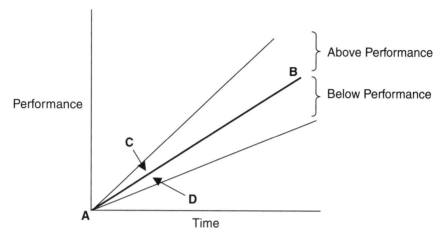

Figure 6-3. The Gap Chart.

The Gap Chart goals:

- To measure performance other than revenue
- To observe work output and make early corrections, both positive and negative
- To allow the salespeople to measure themselves against a necessary goal that is a measure of their real success

Gap Charts are a powerful way for you to measure the quality of work that a salesperson or a sales team needs to exhibit. You should have three to five Gap Charts per review session. Gap-Chart measurements could include different goals for different people.

Salesperson

- New sales
- Prospects contacted
- Forecast accuracy
- Certain product sales

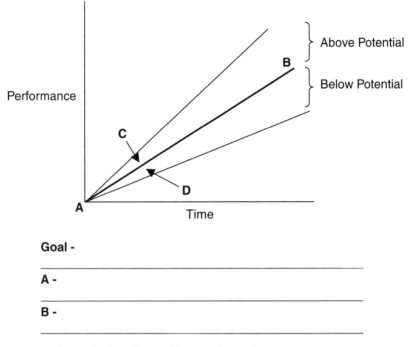

Goal -
_____

A -
_____

B -
_____

Figure 6-4. A sample Gap Chart with room for goals.

- Presentations made
- Customers visited

Sales Manager

- Team goal achievement
- CRM forecast accuracy
- New sales percent
- Certain product sales
- Hiring efficiency
- Employee retention

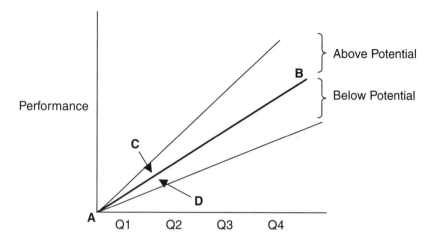

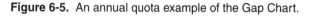

Goal—Last year, Bob did $1.2M. This year, his goal is $1.5M.

A—Last year Bob did $1.2M, added 15 new accounts, and had a monthly forecast accuracy of 85 percent.

B—This year, Bob's goal is $1.5M, 20 new-named accounts, and a monthly forecast accuracy of 88 percent.

C—At the end of the first quarter, Bob should have sold $350K and have 3 new named customers. The upside Gap is $400K and 4 new customers.

D—The downside Gap is $320K, less than $310K, and fewer than 2 new-named customers.

Figure 6-5. An annual quota example of the Gap Chart.

There is no end to what the Gap Charts can measure, and the goal here is to measure the items that predict overall performance. Stop having reviews based on revenue and sales progress per customer. Be predictive in your meetings. Use Gap Charts.

The job of the sales manager is to make the future more attainable.

The battle is won or lost before
the first shot is fired.
—SUN TZU, *THE ART OF WAR*

Not to draw military analogies to the sales function, but this statement is true. If you have the best-trained sales team, ProActive compensation, metrics that focus on the behavior you feel is necessary to accomplish the objectives, and the ability to note the performance gaps early, you and your team win.

PART TWO

UPWARD DECISIONS

"Experience is the name everyone gives to their mistakes."
—OSCAR WILDE (1854–1900), *LADY WINDERMERE'S FAN,* ACT III

CLDs. Career-limiting decisions. You have been exposed to them, seen some-one make one, and maybe have made one yourself. CLDs are different from CADs (career-advancing decisions), which are good—and have a tendency to be few and far between.

In sales management, it is always a good CAD to communicate upward. Most sales managers agree with this concept. The problem is, no one really understands the sales organization but the people in sales, just like no one really understands finance but the finance people. So when forecast accuracy slips, or certain deals do not come in, or salespeople complain, or rocks are thrown at marketing, engineering, accounting, and the like, or when cus-tomer issues have a major impact on sales, why is it in the best interest of sales management to speak up?

It is critical for the sales department and the rest of the organization to communicate because sales controls the company's revenue. If sales isn't talk-ing to the rest of the company, or it's leaving out critical information or provok-ing an "Us versus Them" attitude, danger is on the horizon.

So, chapters 7 through 11 present several communication mistakes that real sales managers have made. Hopefully, you can learn something from their faux pas.

My Management Lets Me Do My Job

"I'm running this show."
—FAMOUS LAST WORDS

Sometimes, sales managers feel like they are king of the kingdom. Small detail . . . there are bigger kings.

GIVE THEM WHAT THEY WANT TO HEAR

Everybody loves to hear good news. Heck, you can obtain near-hero status with reports of increased revenue, increased margins, full pipelines, and statistics showing you're the market leader. These reports make everyone proud, and the people who produce those numbers really do deserve a pat on the back.

But want a kick in the butt? Report that you missed a revenue goal. Report that margins are down, returns are high, customers are leaving in droves, and the pipeline is empty. Who wants to report that? Keep reporting bad news and you get help, and, usually, help is a bad thing. So you learn to report only good news, and the bad news . . . hmm . . . Don't need any help so let's just cover that next quarter, right? Wrong!

TREAT YOUR BOSS LIKE YOUR CUSTOMER

Why do you treat your boss like a boss? Think about it. You are careful about what you say, always try to put a positive spin on things, and usually are on the defensive. With a customer, yes, you do watch what you say, but you are more on the offensive. You point out both the upside and the downside to decisions. You play offense and defense at all times, which is good because you can see things from all perspectives. And seeing things this way keeps you from hitting major potholes.

ASK, AND YOU WILL BE WAY AHEAD

Sales managers are an independent lot. Because most sales managers came up from the sales ranks, they actually think they have earned the right to run the sales organization without any inside influence. Heck, if you "never carried a bag," how can you possibly know what sales is all about, right? That's like saying to a customer, "Well, because you have never bought from *me* before, how could I possibly know what you want?" Seems a bit stupid, doesn't it?

Most bosses have an idea of how they want their functional areas to run. Asking your boss how to run your function is not wise. It's like asking a customer, "What would you like to buy?"

But asking the boss or bosses, "What are your goals for sales in the upcoming year?" is a great question. It's like asking your customers what their goals are for the upcoming year. You can make sure you understand the lay of the land.

Most sales managers seem to think that asking for help is a sign of weakness. Really, it is a sign of strength. Just think of your boss for a second. He or she has a role for you and your responsibilities. Don't you think it's a good idea to ask for feedback—let's say once a quarter—to make sure you are both in sync?

Nope. What happens is that sales management goes upstairs and delivers a presentation on what it is doing. Isn't this the same "show up and throw up" behavior sales management is telling its salespeople *not* to exhibit?

"Hey, no spray and pray. No show up and throw up. Ask what they want before you give them our pitch. Learn to listen."

—Famous words of advice to salespeople from sales management

Treat your boss better than a boss. Treat your boss like a customer. Use the skills you have acquired over the years. Do not let them atrophy. It's a waste of talent, and you are not doing what you're telling your sales organization to do. Go figure.

MANAGE RISK AND GAPS

So, what can you do to effectively communicate to your bosses—yes, you have multiple bosses—so that they give you valuable input and feel they have contributed and have been heard, and you feel like you get to do your thing? Just like in sales, it's all about value, risk, and gaps.

Welcome to the Gap Charts for managers. They're the same charts you use for your team, but they serve as a vehicle for you to communicate upward.

Let's face it. Usually, there are two or three things every quarter that are really important. The rest is not just noise, but every quarter, there are those few items that need attention. These are the items you apply to Gap Charts (see Figure 7-1). Now, because you are a manager and you need to be thinking a bit further out than a few months, Gap Charts for managers have a time element to them—and therefore a risk element.

The Gap Charts for managers are not forms. You will not be showing up at a meeting with 14 Gap Charts and going through them slide by slide. The Gap Charts are a communication vehicle. They're a way for you to get input—yes, even get help—and stay in charge of your sales organization.

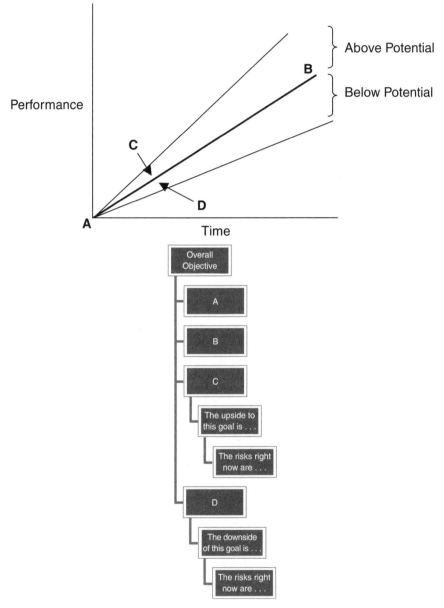

Figure 2-2. The sales productivity curve.

M I S T A K E

I'm the Boss

"Sales managers forget about company intradepartment
dependencies and want to "manage" the sales team.
They believe they are in charge of revenue."

Why is there a tendency to treat a sales organization like the military or a sports team? Because the language is the same, and some of the tactics are as well. Just consider some of these common phrases:

"There is a battle to be won."

"Hit a home run."

"Go for the extra point."

"Take the high ground."

"If we win this battle, we can win the war."

Sure, the military and sports teams are both competitive and hierarchical, like sales, but there is one crucial difference: the boss.

Now, the boss of a sports team—would that be the coach, the head coach, the owner, the shareholders? The boss of the military—would that be the field commander, the general, the head of the armed forces, or the civilian president? Or how about the voters, who elect the president, who selects the head of the armed forces, who appoints the generals?

When you get down to it, the word *boss* is a bit hazy when applied to the military or to sports teams. Who is the boss in your organization? Well, it isn't you, that's for sure.

IT'S NOT ALL ABOUT THEM, IT'S ABOUT LEVERAGE

Everyone has a boss. You do too. The general rule with bosses is the golden rule:

> **"He who has the gold makes the rules."**

Pretty simple rule. It's the same feeling you have for your subordinates. It's their territory, but it's your team. As long as the team members fall in line with your expectations, you will allow them to do what they say they need to do in their territories, but they need to keep you informed.

How is this different from your relationship with your boss? Here are some common refrains.

- "She really doesn't understand sales. That's why she hired me."

- "They have too many other fires to worry about. They don't need more from me."

- "If I tell them what I am up to, they will want to give me a suggestion. And it's tough not to act on a suggestion from the boss—and even tougher to convince him that he is not exactly right."

The list goes on and on. Here's a hint: It's not *your* sales team; it's the company's sales team. You just happen to be holding the reins for a while. As a responsible member of the management team, your goal is to have the company run the sales team, and by doing this, you create leverage.

How?

Well, the management team that runs sales runs the rest of the company, right? So now you get to dabble in finance, manufacturing, consulting, marketing, engineering, and everything else that can hold sales back. Sales is the only—repeat, the *only*—function in a company that has an external boss: the customer.

Now, other departments can say they are responsible to the customer too, and they would be right. But let's say the engineering department wants to build a product over the protests of the customer, and let's say the product doesn't sell. Who will take the hit? Not engineering. I know of a company whose product caught on fire in test mode at a beta customer site. *It caught on fire*. Sales were delayed six months and the company did not make its revenue goal for the year. The VP of sales left, but the VP of engineering stayed on. Go figure.

The answer is for you to help create a working culture that allows the bottom line and the customer to drive the company. The terms are not mutually exclusive.

How do you do this? You take the company to the customer.

For example, when was the last time all senior management sat through a focus group, worked a booth at a trade show, or made a series of customer visits? You, as the leader of the sales team, can make that happen. It creates a more market-centric company and, most important, creates leverage. There are more wheels going in the same direction.

● CASE STUDY ●

There are two ways of thinking about the role of sales managers in companies: the old way and the new way.

The Old Way

In the old way of thinking, we find the sales manager, or the sales VP, "in charge." And why shouldn't we? No one else carried a bag. No one else can do the things that are required to make the quarterly numbers. It's all played out in front of everybody. There's no place to hide, and that scares too many people. It's why sales managers consider themselves kings of their domain. No one else has the top line in mind like sales does, so if you are in charge of sales, you are the boss. Pretty simple theory.

The New Way

The new way of thinking revolves around the idea that the company owns the sales function. The sales-management team is in charge of execution. Goals are now set monthly instead of just annually. Fewer grenades are thrown and fewer fingers are pointed. Sales strategies are discussed; sales tactics are not. Goals are passed down to the first-line managers in order to have total buy-in. Leverage is created. How? With many people focused on a combined task, the probability of success is much higher.

Example #1

Two companies are installing a CRM/SFA system. Company #1, which we'll call Dallas, is purchasing the system it feels will get the job done. It has also hired an outside consulting firm to help with installation and training. Some of the salespeople and sales managers have seen a demo of the system. They like it; they think it is the most useable one for their needs. Their IT department was brought in to make sure it is compatible with the current IT environment.

Company #2 (we'll call it Chicago) needs to automate its sales team as well. It put a team of people together from the IT, sales, finance, marketing, customer service, and purchasing departments. The company developed a phased approach that allowed all members of the team to be involved, but not actively involved, until their specialty areas were up for review. For example, the team members from the finance department were not actively involved in system demos, but they were actively involved in the terms and conditions. Because they were involved (albeit to a lesser degree) from the start, the time they spent "getting up to speed" was minimal, and all team members were on the same page.

Example #2

Dallas wanted to implement a major-account program. It brought in the sales-management team, which looked at the data, considered the people it had in the field, made its decision, and then went to the rest of the company to sell the idea.

Chicago got all the functional departments together and stated the long-term and short-term objectives, as well as its views of the market. All team members were active in setting three-month goals for transitioning the company from a one-tiered sales team to a two-tiered sales team, and the VP of marketing was the lead on this plan, not the VP of sales. The sales VP had more important execution items to pay attention to and felt good about the delegation.

Analysis. As with the military and sport teams, there are no clear-cut bosses with Dallas, and the bosses who play well with one another (like in Chicago) usually win. The game is not "I'm in charge." It's "How can we get everyone to win?"

Leverage is getting the whole team to play together, with you being the leader. What you do affects everyone in the organization. You just have to think in a "leverage way" instead of a "sales and revenue way."

————• CREATING A PROACTIVE CULTURE •————

Here is a hint regarding cultures:

> "Cultures are top down. Change is bottom up."
> —BILL UNDERWOOD, CEO, CATALYST CONSULTING TEAM

Bill is a friend of mine who does some organizational consulting. He is one of the brightest people I know. We have looked at sales cultures and have made the following observations:

- *Look from the top down.* Sales cultures are directly related to the person at the top of the sales team, be it the senior vice president or the first-line sales manager. Given that, they are proactive with their top-down and bottom-up communication.

- *Listen.* What great sales cultures have in common is their ability to listen to change from the bottom up.

- *Say yes.* Great sales cultures look for ways to do things; they want to know how new ideas will work, not why they won't work.

- *Get out of the way.* Great sales cultures understand that the manager's sales paradigm is what usually holds people back, and they take proactive steps to get out of the way, even if the manager believes it is not the best "choice."

• *Own the process.* The sales team that owns the buy/sales process wins. Companies that do not have a sales process defined by the company and executed from the salespeople all the way through to the management level usually sell on price. And they usually fail.

• *Measure.* The strength of the sales team is the ability of the first-line sales managers to implement and measure. Good first-line managers equal success. Bad first-line managers equal work in progress.

People who head sales teams know they cannot do it alone, and they actively recruit their subordinates, peers, and bosses to redefine cultures.

Protecting the Reps

Ron just heard the news . . .

Ron is a divisional sales manager whose team sells what their division produces, and there are two other divisions, so there is some cross-selling going on.

The news Ron has just heard is that there is going to be a contest for the reps who can sell multiple divisions' products between now and the end of the year. This decision is not good, on many levels. Ron thinks the effort to sell multiple products will be more than it's worth.

It's time to help the reps, so Ron has decided that he will make sure his reps fully understand that if they sell more of the other divisions' products, it will hurt them in the pocketbook, as well as hurt the team. Help company, hurt team.

The problem with Ron is that he thinks he speaks for the team. Change is bottom up, and if the sales team is any good, it will figure it out soon enough. Ron's old way of managing has made Ron look bad not only to his peers and bosses, but to his sales team as well. The team does not believe Ron has the faith, trust, and confidence to figure it out. The sales team will now depend on Ron for everything; Ron will stay happy because he is in control.

The dependent reps are happy; the A reps will leave.

Ron, you are not the boss, and by protecting your reps, you have told them to depend on you, and they will. The ones who work most effectively, the A players, do not want your "help" and they will move on.

MANAGE FOR INTERDEPENDENCIES

It's all about managing for interdependencies—creating leverage, being proactive about culture and change, and letting the team learn and grow—not "protecting" team members from themselves.

Things Are Always Tough at the End of the Quarter

"The end of the quarter is what it is."

Here are a few other famous phrases associated with that notorious three-month benchmark:

- "Our customers are conditioned to buy at the end of a quarter."

- "The hockey stick has been around as long as I can remember."

- "If people think they can take vacations at the end of the quarter, they are working for the wrong company."

- "Three days left and then I can go home to my family."

Why do sales managers always seem to let their sales teams come down to the end of the month, or quarter, or year when it comes to meeting sales goals? What causes the sales team to be so stressed at the end of a quarter, when the buyer has no stress at all?

For sales managers who have come out of the dark and have taken control of their sales forecasts and funnel management, getting rid of their hockey-stick sales-management culture is one of the best things they could have done.

This mistake, managing to the end of the month, quarter, or year (now called managing to the calendar), is not mentioned by many in our survey, but to the ones who brought it up, it is very high. Why? For one thing, buyers are annoyed by having to buy products or services based on the sales team's schedule. But more important, it's a matter of being reactive versus ProActive.

There is no need to bring up the differences between the two styles. But it should be noted that reactive sales teams push; they sling their stuff—and they wonder why they end up selling on price. This is not a bad thing, really. If you are in a market-share grab, a commodity play, or trying to set a new paradigm and cut sales cycles in half, it may not be a bad idea. If your culture needs a sense of urgency, this would be a reason to push as well.

However, most sales teams are in a reactive trap—with no clue how to get out. Here are some clues.

THE SALESPERSON'S PERCEPTION, AND HOW TO BREAK IT

It's all about attention, right? Praise, reward, recognition—that's what will get you noticed by the important people, and then it's promotion time. Did you ever notice who gets the rewards?

Imagine this scenario:

1. It's 10 days into the quarter, and Jill closes her biggest deal of the year.

2. It's six hours before end of quarter, and John closes the same-size deal as Jill did three months ago.

Now ask yourself these questions:

1. Who gets the rewards?

2. Who is in line to win the contest you put together two weeks ago so the quarter could go out with a bang?

3. Who is in line for a call from the president?

4. Who is in line for a promotion?

5. Who is going to do the same thing next quarter?

6. Who is going to wait until the end of the quarter to close business from now on?

Salespeople will do what you ask them to do. If you want them to close business earlier, then set up the goals and objectives to do just that. It's time for:

- Better forecast accuracy

- Customer-centric forecasting

- Objectives that are measured to the beginning of the month or quarter rather than the end

Salespeople are usually told, in no uncertain terms, that they are to wait until the end of the month/quarter before they should start doing any heavy lifting.

THE CUSTOMER'S PERCEPTION: I-DATES AND DRAGONS

You now have the idea that customer-set dates are better than *your* dates. If the sales team had solid forecasts, based on when the customer was really going to buy, how much would that be worth to you?

Look at the time line in Figure 9-1. If A is the start of a sale, what happens at B?

A |————————————————▶| **B**

Figure 9-1. The customer time line.

At point B, one might assume the customer:

- Signs the check

- Cuts the purchase order (P.O.)

- Executes the agreement

But that's not even close. At point B the customer actually begins using your product or service. Signing the order happens at about point C, as shown in Figure 9-2.

Figure 9-2. The customer time line marking time C.

But think about it: Do you really care about when you *bought* your TV, or do you care about when you plan to *use* it? Do you care about when you bought your vacation or when you will take it? You can bet the travel agent could care less when you go. He cares about when you buy the vacation. Same with your customers: All they care about is point B, which is called an implementation date, or I-Date (see Figure 9-3).

Figure 9-3. The customer time line to the implementation date.

The I-Date is what your customers make their decisions around. If your sales team would focus on these dates, rather than "When are we getting the P.O.?", you might be heading toward a ProActive culture and away from a reactive one.

An additional note: an I-Date is not any good without Dragons. A Dragon is a commitment, an event, an action, an expenditure, anything that anchors that I-Date. Here are some examples of how I-Dates and Dragons interact.

- The date someone is going to purchase a car is tied to the day she has to turn in her car at the end of the lease.

- More television sets are sold the week before the Super Bowl.

- Your customer has made a commitment to shut down a plant the first week of next month. If it does not have your product by then, the shutdown will have to be rescheduled, which may cause hardship.

There should always be two Dragons for every I-Date. Once you know the commitments the customer has made, you'll be working to meet customer dates instead of arbitrary dates (from the customer's point of view). Your calendar-based sales efforts will tend to go away.

THE MANAGER'S PERCEPTION— GO FORWARD, NOT BACKWARD

As you can tell, the manager's perception goes a long way in feeding the end-of-calendar frenzy. If the manager believes there is an end-of-month or end-of-quarter paradigm, then that's exactly what will happen. If a manager manages the business by monitoring weekly or monthly activity, not results, then the end-of-the-calendar periods won't seem so crazy.

It's Always Been Like This

Our business has always been quarter-driven. Our salespeople believe it, our customers believe it, and our industry believes it. Our customers wait until the end of the quarter to get a better deal, and because 70 percent of our business is renewal business, this has a major impact on sales margin.

So one time, my Southwest manager had enough. He told his salespeople he was not going to discount any deal. When the customers came asking, the standard line was to be, 'We used to discount, but we have new management now, and we do not do that anymore.'

We closed 18 deals in the quarter, and 16 came in either at list price or at a 5 percent discount or less, compared to the previous quarter when the average deal was discounted 32 percent. Seems we were the ones causing the discount, nothing else.

This story has been told a few times, and disbelief is usually the reaction. About five others come to mind if you want to listen to them, but they all carry the same lesson: Dependence on the end-of-calendar crunch comes from poor management practices that use artificial dates for motivational purposes. Heck, it's easy to use "end of quarter" or "end of month" as a rallying cry. It makes "logical" sense.

Please understand that you should not take away this motivation if it is working. The point is that if you are using end-of-period motivation by itself, you may be:

- Stressing out your sales team unnecessarily

- Giving more discounts than you need to and therefore negatively affecting margins

- Creating a beast you may have a hard time getting rid of

During our research, one particular manager spoke about his first 30 days on the job. He has had three sales VP jobs in the past eleven years, all of them turnarounds. He gets in, helps turn it around, and then finds another one. He likes the risk and the stock he gets. Here is his story.

One of the first things I do when I am new to a sales-management position is to stop the sales team from discounting. They usually are discounting 10 to 70 percent. Yep, in some cases 70 percent, and the sales team has every rationalized reason why they need to do this. For two quarters, discounts go to zero, and we may lose some business, but we'll still win a lot. Then we'll allow some discounts, up to 10 or 12 percent, and then it's back to business as usual, but revenue and margins are healthier. Then I identify the end-of-the-quarter rush, where salespeople want to get a deal at 50 percent off to make the quarter. I then start working on that issue.

•————• MICROMANAGE—SPEED KILLS •————•

How often have you heard this? "I like my bosses; they leave me alone to do my job."

Not any more. It's time to reevaluate the topic of micromanagement. Not the type where you are asking the salespeople what's closing every ten minutes. That "inquisition" style of sales management should still be dead. What works? Effective time management.

Speed kills. You go too fast, you get in trouble; go too slow and you will miss the opportunity. The modulation of speed is now in the hands of sales management. Look at this idea as a matrix involving speed and priorities—an SPMatrix.

Speed/Priority = SPMatrix

This SPMatrix is not another tool you sit down with your sales rep and go over. There are already enough tools. The SPMatrix in Figure 9-4 happens to be a 3×3 matrix. You can have up to a 7×7 or even a 6×3. Do not limit yourself by making it a size issue.

The SPMatrix in Figure 9-4 was put together by a manager who had just come off a bad quarter. (Here is that end-of-quarter thing again.) It seems he had a team of managers and salespeople who made a break for the end of the quarter, said they had 140 percent of what they needed in the funnel, and then came up at 83 percent for the quarter. Sound familiar? Anyway, the manager looked at what happened and what was needed, and he built the matrix.

		Speed		
		Month 1	Month 2	Month 3
Priority	Top	AA	AB	AC
	Middle	BA	BB	BC
	Possible	CA	CB	CC

Figure 9-4. The SPMatrix.

The question now was what to focus on. He came up with the reasons he missed the quarter.

1. Bad qualification skills

2. Not getting to the right decision maker

These items went into the AA bucket. The team needed to come up with some guidelines so all deals would be held accountable to these new metrics. He then thought of what he needed to do to make sure this would never happen again.

1. Take action on two C reps.

2. Start interviewing process using Profile Sheets.

3. Get together with A reps and find out what is really available for them to close.

4. Get decisions on last quarter's business (the stuff that did not close from the last quarter) so the team can focus on this quarter's business.

5. Increase average sales price (ASP) on deals that are being quoted.

6. Assess overall team strengths and create a contest around these items.

The list had about 15 items. He assigned a matrix value to each priority.

1. Take action on two C reps—AA

2. Start interviewing process using Profile Sheets—AA

3. Get together with A reps and find out what is really available for them to close—AB

4. Get decision on last quarter's business (the stuff that did not close from the last quarter) so the team can focus on this quarter's business—BA

5. Increase average sales price (ASP) on deals that are being quoted—BB

6. Assess overall team strengths and create a contest around these items—CA

The SPMatrix produces a workable list, right in front of you, of what has to happen by when. It's like a New Year's resolution that you write up in January and don't look at again until December. However, the SPMatrix is monthly, and because it is a visual, you leave it right on your desk or post it on your wall and communicate it to your boss and your subordinates to make sure everyone knows what you are working on. (Note: If you are going to take action on a C player, you may not want to show that SPMatrix to the sales team. Use good judgment!) Figure 9-5 shows on example of the SPMatrix in action.

The purpose of the SPMatrix is to provide a visual model of where you should ProActively spend your time. The SPMatrix minimizes the end-of-the-calendar crunch. Some of the world's best sales managers use it to manage their time—and so should you. Otherwise your time may end up managing you.

Speed

		July	August	September
Priority	Top	AA Action on C Reps Profile Sheets	AB A Rep Meeting	AC
	Middle	BA Last Q Business	BB Increase ASP	BC
	Possible	CA Strength Contest	CB	CC

Figure 9-5. A sample SPMatrix.

10

It's All About Revenue

The thinking goes like this.

* When it's all over, what's the final score? Who won the game?

* No one ever asks you what percent of quota you were for the year.
  All they ask you is: Did you make the club?

THE GOLDEN MEASURE IS REVENUE

It's all about revenue. No sales VP ever got fired for being 120 percent of
quota. No coach was ever asked to leave after finishing the season 12–1
and also winning the conference championship. It's all about the final
result.

Great, but how did you get there? Sales managers can get so caught up
in the final result that they trip, stumble, and fall along the way. They may
get there, but the carnage in their wake makes it even harder next year. It's
about the planning and the metrics. It's not only the execution that really
counts.

———————• WHAT MAKES UP REVENUE •———————

My son is a high school quarterback. He loves throwing the football and throwing it long. He does it very well. So one day, his coach asked him a question: "What's the primary job of a quarterback?"

Well there is an easy answer, thought my son. "To win the game," he said.

"Nope," said the coach. "There are 40 players on the team, 6 coaches, and a host of other people. They have to win the game. Try again."

"Okay, to score as many points as possible."

"Nope," said the coach again. "There are 11 players on offense, an offensive coordinator, and others too. Try again."

Sensing a trick, my son replied, "To be the best quarterback and leader I can be."

"Not really. You see, with that attitude, you will be good, you will lead, but will others follow and reach their potential?"

Now clearly frustrated, my son said, "Well, I don't know then."

"Good," said the coach. "With that attitude, we can start at the beginning. If you want to know what the job of the quarterback is, look down at the field. What do you see?"

"I see a football field," said the quarterback.

"What else do you see?"

"I see lines and numbers."

"Very good, now what do those lines and numbers mean?"

"They measure how successful you are."

"Very good answer. Now, during a game, how can you tell if you are doing a good job?"

"I look at the sideline chains. They tell me what I have to do."

"You win," said the coach. "The goal of the quarterback is to move the chains by taking a snap, handing off, using head fakes, passing, or by running the ball. Whatever it takes to move those chains is your job. When you move the chains a lot more than the other team, guess what happens?"

"You win."

"Mr. Quarterback," he called him. "Your job is to move the chains."

From that point forward, my son started working on a lot more than just throwing the ball. He worked on all the things it took to move the chains.

What are you doing to move the chains—week by week, month by month, so you will win more often than you lose? It is not about the final score. It's getting to that final score by being in the right position at the right time in the right place.

How? By keeping the team motivated and measuring the right things. It's not just a revenue game anymore.

HOW TO KEEP A MOTIVATED SALES TEAM

The scoreboard. The final score. Sales organizations use revenue to motivate.

"Larry, your team is at 77 percent of plan year-to-date. What are you going to do about it?"

"Bob, you are 122 percent year-to-date. That makes three quarters in a row that you have been over plan. Why are you doing so well? Put together a presentation for next week's staff meeting, will you?"

"Cheryl, at 96 percent of your number, your region is so close. Let's get out there and break 100 percent."

Is this really going to motivate, or just supply status? It's typical sales-management talk; however, the manager or salesperson will leave the room with a question: What specifically am I going to do about it?

The specifics of what needs to get done are important, but so are tapping into the employee's or team's motivation. For sales types, those motivations are:

- To learn and grow
- To be challenged

LEARN AND GROW

Survey after survey finds that salespeople want to be in organizations that are committed to a "learn-and-grow philosophy" for their people. This is one thing sales management needs to work on every month and every quarter. It's not just about the revenue; it's about the need for learning and growing.

Why are Internet search engines, social networking, and business information sites so popular? Because people, salespeople included, have a need for learning and exploring. They also have this desire to grow, to try new things, get promoted, and be rewarded for their growth. In promoting their "learn-and-grow" cultures, winning organizations have:

- Made sure they spend between 3 and 15 percent of their budgets on formalized training.

- Kept business libraries in the forefront of the sales organization.

- Made sure their organizations have easy access to business information from sources such as Hoovers.com.

- Instituted monthly brown-bag lunch-and-learns.

- Invested in technology to stay abreast of the current trends. (Essentially, every three to four years, your company's technology needs a major overhauling or should be replaced. Such is the nature of the beast.)

The list can go on and on. You and your organization need to sponsor a learn-and-grow culture. How are you doing this today? By not doing this, you are making a huge mistake, as other sales managers have found out.

● CHALLENGE ●

One of the most famous sayings about sales is, "Salespeople want to learn and grow, and their touchstone is challenge." Other famous quotes include:

"You can't do that."

"No one can do that."

"Steve tried that a few years ago, and he couldn't make it work."

Give a salesperson a challenge and watch that person ignite. Not all salespeople will run to be No. 1, but all salespeople have a challenge they need to face. Challenges in overcoming fears are very popular, but interestingly, most salespeople do not want to face a challenge by themselves. Give them a team atmosphere or an audience, and now you can watch them grow.

Learn and Grow?

A pretty large organization was going through a major sales change. It was going to shift resources to pursue more global and national accounts. This was going to require a major investment of resources.

There were three things the organization was going to address first: sales strategy, the sales organization's fit with the strategy, and training.

The team assigned to executing this shift spent weeks focusing on a sales strategy and how to meet the organization's and customers' needs. Round and round they went, and they finally believed they had a working model.

Time for the training piece. They identified the types of training and retraining they were going to need. Then someone asked, "Are we going to get our internal sales-training organization involved with this?"

Dead silence was met with lowered heads. After about 20 seconds, someone asked if the sales-management team should be involved with the retraining of the sales team.

Groans were met with blank stares.

Finally, the team realized that if it did not involve the company's training organization and sales-management team, and hold them accountable for the success of any training effort, it was going to fail. Saved by the bell.

Give George another headline, and he's
good for another thirty miles.

—QUOTE FROM THE MOVIE *PATTON*

What are you doing, besides measuring revenue, to challenge your sales team?

THE TRUE MEASURE OF A SUPERSTAR

What is your definition of *superstar*? Anyone who makes quota? Someone who tries her hardest? A salesperson who does the "impossible" and makes a great sale?

Doing it again and again and again: That's what separates the one-year wonder from the rest of the lot. Real superstars use their strengths to stay on top. As a manager, your job is to reward performance; your goal is for your sales team to become individual superstars. Most managers are great at rewarding for revenue, but measuring and rewarding the things that make a team or an individual a superstar is not often in the cards.

Well, it's time you started measuring and rewarding your team for the efforts that will make them superstars.

The Revenue = F+C+T Formula

Let's assume you have a $10 million quota for the year. It could be $1 million, $1 billion—whatever your number is for the year.

Congratulations! You have had some problems in your company, and now you need to do 15 percent more than your quota. How will you do it? Beat your sales team? Sell them on the idea? Fight and scream to your bosses that it cannot be done?

Let's treat this as a math problem. What are the variables? Screaming and shouting are not really good variables, as good as they make you feel sometimes. The three variables you have at your disposal are:

1.   Frequencies

2.   Competencies

3.   Time

These are the only three variables you can use to solve your revenue problem. They're all you have going for you. Why? Because these are the only things you can control and modify that will have a direct result on revenue. These are the variables that ProActively make up revenue. Let's take a look at each.

Frequencies. This includes the number of:

Calls made   Calls made to senior-level people

Prospecting calls   Prospecting dials

Prospecting meetings	Presentations
Presentations to higher-level titles	Demonstrations
TripTiks	Proposals
Senior internal meetings	In-person visits
WebEx meetings	Plant tours

There are a host of items you can measure. Pick the five or six you feel are the most important for the next six months, or make up your own list and measure your team on those. Every month or two, delete one and then add one that you feel is the most important for your team to accomplish for the near future. By focusing on frequencies or activities, you can be assured your team will be doing the right things.

Then, to personalize it, add one or two unique measurable items to the lists you make for each of your team. That way, everyone will have the core list of frequencies, but every individual will have one or two items tailored to what that person specifically needs to accomplish.

Competencies. What do you do to get your team better? Where does it need to get better? Over the next six to nine months, what does it need to improve? Consider these items.

Selling skills	Presentation skills
Prospecting skills	Qualifying skills
Calling-high skills	Negotiating skills
Telephone skills	Territory management
E-mail skills	Closing skills
Coaching skills	Hiring skills
Motivation skills	Interviewing skills
Leadership skills	Time-management skills

The list can go on and on; however, you need to be the judge of what skills are needed based on what the organization needs to get done.

Time. You've heard the phrase "Speed Kills." Go too fast, you burn up; go to slow and you will be left behind. What are you doing to change the time element of your organization? Consider these ideas.

Faster training schedule	Shorter sales-cycle length
Longer senior sales visits	Shorter qualification time
Shorter demonstration	Longer homework
Longer time in two-way education	More time with top 10 accounts
Less time with renewal accounts	Less time with prospects over 30 days old
Sales cycle time	Improved get-to-proposal time
Improved speed of communication	Improved timeliness of corrective action
Improved speed of change	Improved speed of meetings
Improved speed of delegation	Improved speed of decisions
Improved timeliness of hiring	

In my previous book, *ProActive Sales Management,* I introduce the Miller 17 tool, which uses frequencies and competencies to measure performance. It is probably the most-used tool in that book. You can add Time to that list and have a "Miller 17/t," which would work perfectly.

Figure 10-1 is an example of a Miller 17. There are 10 items, not 17. That's OK. This example includes reviews for five individuals. The scale goes from one to five, where five means the employee is doing what needs to be done, and one means a serious discussion needs to take place.

● **MILLER 7** ●

If speed is indeed one of the rules right now in the sales-management game, then the Miller 7 is the tool to use. Coaching to things other than revenue is a key variable when getting an A employee to A+ status (or getting any employee better for that matter). The annual employee-performance review is a

Second Quarter Reviews					
1–5 Scale (1 = Low – 5 = Excellent)					
PERFORMANCE	**2.5**	**2.5**	**1.5**	**3.5**	**3.5**
SALES QUARTER REVIEW	2	3	2	4	2
NEW SALES	3	2	1	3	5
SALES COMPETENCY	**3.0**	**4.0**	**2.0**	**3.0**	**5.0**
SALES CYCLE CONTROL	3	4	2	2	5
PRESENTATION SKILLS	3	4	2	4	5
FREQUENCY	**4.0**	**3.7**	**2.0**	**3.0**	**5.0**
ACCOUNT PENETRATION	2	3	2	4	5
FIELD TIME MAXIMIZATION	5	4	2	2	5
CALLS PER WEEK	5	4	2	3	5
TIME	**1.3**	**1.7**	**2.3**	**2.3**	**2.3**
SALES CYCLE TIME	2	2	3	5	4
NEW PRODUCT INTRODUCTIONS	3	3	3	4	4
INCREASING ASP	1	2	4	3	3

Figure 10-1. An example of the Miller 17.

good tool, but when it's out of sight, it's out of mind. The Miller 7 is a better tool for changing short-term behavior.

The Miller 7 (so named because my last name is Miller and the tool's term is seven weeks) identifies the one or two frequencies, competencies, or time element(s) in which you want an employee to improve. The tool (see Figure 10-2) keeps these items at center stage for seven weeks and then allows employees the freedom to tailor the new skill to their personal style.

To use the Miller 7, you start by looking at the employee's performance and what you believe is needed to get this employee or team further than it is today. You write down these specific goals. Then you remind the employee of his strengths. When employees are aware of the strengths they can summon to get to the next level, reaching the desired outcome is easier.

Once Goals and Strengths have been worked out, you track the employee's progress through a series of goals you and the employee set on a weekly basis. This will allow the employee ample time to modify her behavior in a

Employee Name _____ **Manager** _____
Date _____

Goals	Strengths
M²O/t Week 1	M²O/t Week 2
M²O/t Week 3	M²O/t Week 4
M²O/t Week 5	M²O/t Week 6
Overall Assessment	Next Steps

Final Date _____ **Signed** _____

Figure 10-2. The Miller 7.

positive, coaching manner. And once they accomplish the small weekly tasks, employees can see progress when they decide to look at the bigger picture. It is a perfect way to take a situation, cut it up into bite-size pieces, and then let the employee take ownership.

After seven weeks, give a final assessment, either positive or negative; identify the next steps (if any), sign the tool, and you are done.

Here are some ground rules for the Miller 7.

- The Miller 7 can be used for an employee, a sales team, or a matrix sales team calling on a major account.

- Use the tool on one employee or team at a time.

- Set an appointment in advance to review a Miller 7. It should not take longer than 10 minutes per week to review a prepared Miller 7.

- Pick a goal or an objective that is within the F, C, or T guidelines. For example, "Increase revenue by 10 percent" is a great goal, but what specifically do you want the employee to do to get there? That is what the Miller 7 is for.

- You have to be the one who follows up and initiates. This is a management tool, not an employee tool.

- Be positive. Focusing on what the employee cannot do or is not doing will just reinforce that negative behavior.

Figure 10-3 is an example of a partially completed Miller 7.

Employee Name _____ **Manager** _____
Date _____

Goals—These are two goals the employee needs to focus on:
    More time with senior-level buyers
    Better prospecting skills
	Strengths—The employee has great determination and has done very well with senior-level buyers before. Has shown a desire and a commitment to prospect more.

M²O/t Week 1—Contact 3 Vice presidents and get one to commit to a presentation	M²O/t Week 2—Goals for week one accomplished. Same goals for week 1 and get ready for VP presentation.
M²O/t Week 3—Goals for week 2 accomplished. Focus on what you want the buyers to do after the presentation, and contact 3 more VP-level buyers.	M²O/t Week 4
M²O/t Week 5	M²O/t Week 6
Overall Assessment	Next Steps

Final Date _____   **Signed** _____

Figure 10-3. The Miller 7 in action.

Revenue measured by itself will lead the sales manager and the entire sales team down a path of reactive decision making. ProActive measurements will lead to ProActive decisions. It's *your* choice.

PART THREE

SALES DECISIONS

"Mistakes, obviously, show us what needs improving. Without mistakes, how would we know what we had to work on?"
—PETER McWILLIAMS, *LIFE 101*

It's all the same. It's the deal. You know how it is. You were once in sales. The thrill of the hunt, getting the order, bringing home the bacon—it all was worthwhile. You felt good, felt affirmed, and were rewarded. It was a simple life.

Now you are in management, have been for years, and the opportunity for you to be involved in deals ranges from being involved in every deal (heck, it's your sales territory) to not really seeing a customer in two years (i.e., "There is just too much other work to do").

What role should a sales manager take when looking at the sales opportunities? What are the most common mistakes sales management makes regarding sales, especially when the deal is large, it's the end of the quarter, and all eyes are on you?

Mistakes? Oh, there are plenty, and the big four are here in chapters 11 through 15. Have a good read and pay attention; it's only your career.

11

My Team Needs Me for This Important Deal

"Customers want management of the selling company to be involved with major deals. So do our salespeople. So who is really the salesperson?"

It's 5:43 a.m. You are on your home computer checking e-mails. Your spouse and kids will get up soon, and then it starts. This is the only time you have to get something done. By 7:00 a.m., your day is in full swing. You have four e-mails from other time zones where they have already put in a full day. They need your immediate attention. Meanwhile, the kids are up, the dog needs attention, and your 8:00 a.m. meeting is just around the corner.

You get to work at 7:50. At 7:55, one of your midlevel salespeople comes in to your office, panic-stricken, and proclaims: "They are going to make a decision today."

You hope he means the team's decided to leave you alone so you can prepare for your meeting. Fat chance. In fact, he's talking about a somewhat large deal he worked on, left for dead, and then resurrected. The prospect is going to make a decision, and the dollar and quota numbers are starting to form in your head.

You didn't really count on this good-size deal for the quarter. If the prospect makes a decision today, how much work will it take? It may be fun too. It probably will get complicated and will need your involvement. So without hesitation, you utter those words: "Really? What's going on?"

Your day, and probably the rest of the week, will be consumed by this deal. Going after it is part of your job. It will take a lot of effort to bring the prospect into the fold, so you schedule a meeting with the sales-person right after your 8:00 a.m. meeting. Heck, maybe you can leave the meeting early; it's only a planning session for next year.

Sound familiar? Ah yes, we all have choices, and this one may not have been the right one.

NOW VS. FUTURE: LEVERAGE

As a manager, you need to create processes and make decisions that affect the whole organization, just not the parts. If you allow yourself to make individual decisions, you will never get ahead in the race. Quotas are going up, you are going to hire more people, and the decisions seem like they are getting more complex. How do you get ahead? Well, first you have to take a snapshot of where you are.

Leverage is not something you can just wake up and declare you will find today. Your job requires you to be more systematic than that. However, you do not want to get so "ivory tower" that whatever decisions you make have really little or no effect on the sales team. Fine line, you bet.

There are three rules to remember when making decisions about your sales team. The mistakes sales management makes in this area are huge and have cost many their careers or at least their promotions.

Rule #1: 80/20 It

Leverage usually is about customer discounts or what it will take to get a certain deal. You start looking at individual deals, and leverage is lost. Most deals are out of the norm because of poor sales practices, not because the customers want to be hard on you. They know if they are too hard on you, you will take your product elsewhere. It has to be a win-win situation.

The same can be said for management. Leverage can come through decisions about anything from compensation to corrective action to hiring in a remote office. When you are making a decision for the sales team, ask yourself if it will cover 80 percent or more of the decisions in this area. If so, make it. If not, why are you involved?

Look for your decisions to affect 80 percent of the masses as well. If you allow your decisions to get to the 90–95 percent assurance level, you will be spending a great amount of time on a few exceptions. By the way, you are going to treat those exceptions differently when they come up, so why spend so much time with them now? It's all about speed, and 80/20 is a good rule.

Rule #2: Focus on the Future

Did you know that 70 percent of business conversations are focused on the past? The past is full of things you can do nothing about today. Spending so much time talking about them makes no sense. Opportunities abound if you look at where your sales team is going to be rather than where it was. Check yourself and make sure your meetings and decisions are about things in the future.

Getting dragged down in decisions about last week (or even this week) hurts your ability to influence the future. For you, it's all about the next battle. You have to get used to not getting involved in the day-to-day. Sure, it can be fun, but it will cost you.

2+2=?

It's an age-old question with a few good answers, more than the obvious one. If you are a salesperson, the answer is 4. Of course, it is 4. It has to be 4. There is a customer, there is our product. The customer wants to buy it, we want to sell it. It has to be 4. What a revelation.

But the manager has to have a different spin. If she allows the answer to be 4, then she has the same problem with the entire sales team. They all will want to have it equal 4. She will have to face the same problem with every member, and by the time she gets around to every salesperson, more problems arise. It's a never-ending equation, and one that gets old fast. It's really easy to go around to every salesperson and say, "4." Is this her job though? Is this the right answer?

So what is the answer? What does the sales manager have to get to? It depends on the situation. Can 2+2 = 5? How about 6 or 8? What is a good rule of thumb?

Rule #3: Never Forget Rules #1 and #2

Remember the two rules: leverage and future. Look for leverage opportunities and look to the future. So, obviously you need to look for future-based leverage opportunities. To do this, ask yourself these questions.

The Discount

She had just taken over a sales team where 30, 40, and even 50 percent discounts were the norm. It was a subscription business model, where customers were renewing their orders annually. The deals were usually sold with a big discount for the first year, and a "when customers see how valuable we are, they will pay more for the next year" mentality was rampant.

She needed to cut out the discounting but not upset the customer base, which was promised "big discounts." Her rule was simple.

She said, "You go back to those customers and tell them they have to pay more, and their increase has to be in the teens. Fourteen percent, 17 percent, whatever it is, but it has to be a teen increase over what they paid last year."

This rule handled 80 percent of the deals. The other 20 percent was handled on a case-by-case basis, much better than all being handled case by case.

Problem solved. Leverage.

- What commission or compensation opportunity is coming up in which I can get the sales team to prospect for new accounts over and above what they are doing now?

- What is happening this summer/fall/winter/spring that I can take advantage of?

- Is there a market or competitive issue that can cause my sales team to do something different and shake things up a bit?

Stop thinking about current fires; stop thinking about the past. Look to future opportunities and where you can have the most impact. Go on the offensive. Be ProActive.

• GET OUT OF THE OFFICE •

Your team needs you to do this. It makes you ProActive. You can:

- Prospect. Go make a few cold calls and see what it is really like.

- Prospect at a trade show. Man the booth, grab some brochures, and listen to the people who stop by. There will be a lot of useless comments, but there will be some good ones too.

- Visit senior management at your top customers and see what they are up to. You may get some valuable insights on what they are planning to do, not just what they are planning to buy from you.   *yes*

- Speak at an industry event. It's easier than you think. Just call the event organizers and ask. Give them six months' notice and a compelling story and you are there.

- Go on a management tour. Take three or four of your company's top executives to see 10 accounts together. You will get the customers' attention, create goodwill, and learn a lot.   *yes*

● SALES MANAGER VACATION ●

There is nothing like a good vacation to create some leverage. Sure, go on your real vacation, delegate your authority to one or two individuals, and have a good time. You should also go on "minivacations." When you are out of town for a few days on business or for personal reasons, delegate your authority rather than have people try to get hold of you. Turn your Blackberry off. Let them learn and grow.

There is a general rule that more things get done when the manager is on vacation. So go on vacation. A two-day getaway should do it. While you are thinking about the future and looking for leverage points, you are creating additional leverage back at the office.

● COMPETENCY: A DEFINITION ●

You need to work on your competencies now. What could you be doing for the sales organization that would make you better? What competencies would you like to work on? The definition of the competent organization starts with the manager and the management team.

Take your performance today, add in what you think you are going to need to get better at, come up with the final result, and then look at the gap. What are you going to do to narrow the gap? Figure 11-1 can help.

Keep this worksheet close to your desk and look at it at least once a month. If you are not doing something to improve yourself, you are probably not actually helping the team or the organization either. Competency starts at the top.

Managers' Competency Worksheet

What are your three strengths that you possess today as a manager?

1. _____

2. _____

3. _____

What areas need more attention?

1. _____

2. _____

3. _____

A year from now, what new strengths do you want to possess?

1. _____

2. _____

3. _____

Figure 11-1. The managers' competency worksheet.

If you have done your job correctly, the team will not need you for that important deal. It's not about the deal: It is about creating the right culture, the right competencies, and the right motivation. You have to do something better than get in the way of your salespeople. Get out of the way. Go on vacation, create leverage, think of the future, and let the sales team sell.

Sell, Sell, Sell . . . Right?

"What salespeople are given to sell and how buyers buy is different. Managers keep pushing their sales teams to sell, when they should be teaching their sales teams to listen to how the customer wants to buy. It's the idea of *pull versus push* selling."

They call it *sales*, so it makes sense to call the management of it *sales management*, right? Not necessarily. When asked, the sales managers my company has talked to called that nomenclature a big mistake because it implies that the job is to keep the sales team focused on selling techniques. That's okay, but sales management should be about showing sales teams how to get close to the customer, not how to sell *per se*.

This debate is all well and good, except customers do not like to get "sold to"; they like to buy. So the first thing sales management should do is address what is important to the customer. Right up front, it's how customers want to be talked to.

● THREE LANGUAGES ●

Because most companies speak three languages, it's important to make sure your sales team is trilingual. *ProActive Selling* goes through these languages in detail, but it is well worth a discussion here.

Language 1: Userese

The first language is the user language. Whoever is going to be using the product or service is at the first level. This might be the manager, or the director, the user/buyer; it's the person responsible for the day-to-day use of whatever it is you sell.

Language 2: Investmentese

People often use this second language when talking about the investments they are making, the return on the investments, and their overall revenue and expenses. These people are typically in operations or the senior-management level. Most companies call this level "the vice-president level." VPs in each functional group make sure everyone does their share to contribute to revenue and hold the line on expenses. This level has the authority and responsibility to make sure the company directives, which come down from above, are met and exceeded.

Language 3: C-Suitese

The top of the company pecking order is the third level. Here you will find the most senior-level managers, who usually have a C in front of their names. The C stands for *chief*, and these managers are the chiefs of the company: Chief Operating Officer, Chief Financial Officer, Chief Executive Officer, and so on. The C suite has a number of C-level managers, and—like captains on a ship—these people are interested in sighting land. How much land can they get profitably?

These captains have to be in a market that is growing, and they have to grow faster than the market. These are the people who steer the ship into the waters, who know where the voyage is going. They're the ones with the maps to tell them how far they have come, how far they have to go, and if they are in the right ocean.

Figure 12-1 is a visual representation of the content of the three languages.

It is important to know that each level speaks its own language, and if you try to speak language 3 to language-1 buyers, they will have no idea what you are talking about. Speak language 1 to a language-2 buyer, and the buyer will get mad. These language-2 executives spent a long time unlearning language 1, and now they have a new responsibility. If you show up and do not

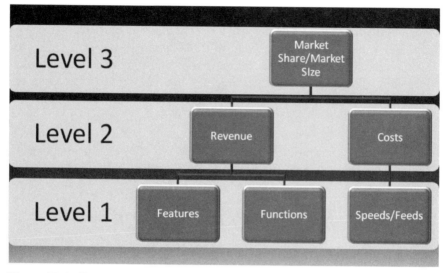

Figure 12-1. The content of the three languages.

respect that responsibility, say, by speaking language 1 to them—well, do not expect great results. Each level of a company speaks its own language, and it is important to make sure your sales team is trilingual. Figure 12-2 is a good example of what this is like.

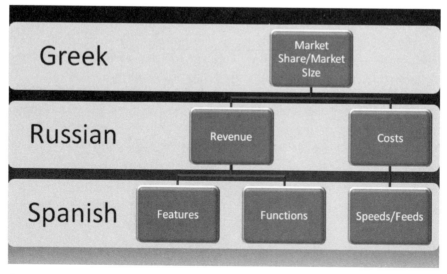

Figure 12-2. An example of the three levels.

Again, this is not one of my ProActive Selling classes, but you do want to make sure your sales team can speak every language. Sales managers who insist their sales teams learn to speak all three languages have seen a 30 percent increase in sales! They use different sales literature or different Power-Point slides. The goals of their meetings are different, and in most cases, the managers who accompany the salesperson for more senior-level calls will have to learn how to speak the top languages too—as opposed to just taking over a sales call to get a deal.

Great sales organizations have their sales and sales-management teams learn the languages so they can speak the customer's "native language."

IT'S ALL ABOUT EXECUTION

Great thoughts exist around sales organizations. That's the problem: They are thoughts. Thoughts without action do not make a successful organization. It's all about execution.

Even the execution of a bad plan can be changed, but what if you can't even get an idea off the ground? Great sales management knows that great ideas start from the ground and go up. The really good ideas begin at the lowest level because these ideas are the ones that are being implemented. In war, it's the soldiers who know what really works on the ground, not the generals. It's the same in business: What changes are the sales and customer service people in your organization clamoring for?

Here is an idea. Have a "change list" on your wall. You are the one who has to implement change, but if nobody signs up to work toward the success of the change, then the possibility of success is pretty low.

When you communicate your change and actually put dates on it, it takes the fear out of the change. It lets the team get comfortable with the change and lets people sign up, because you have now really taken away one of their biggest fears, if not *the* biggest: the fear of the unknown. Figure 12-3 illustrates this idea.

HOW TO START AND END
A SALES CALL

Buyers want to be led.

It is a simple statement, but one that bears great thought from sales management. Most sales teams are more concerned about the content of the sales

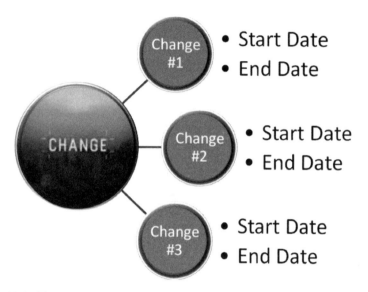

Figure 12-3. The change map.

calls and the sales meetings than the control of the call. It goes back to the reactive theory that if a salesperson does a good job on a sales call, that person will be rewarded by the customer. This reactive thinking is what gets sales organizations in trouble.

It's at the beginning and the end of a call where the control of the call is won or lost. So if you really want to have a ProActive organization, measure performance at the beginning and the end of sales calls, not just the content or the end results. Figure 12-4 shows what I'm talking about.

There are many useful sales tools you can use to start and end sales calls, but it is the job of sales management to measure the successful control of the sale, not just the end results.

Solicit Change

A manager has a Change Map on his wall, and every quarter he solicits input from the organization to revise his Change Map. He gets about 20 to 40 suggestions per quarter, and the ideas that make his list get special attention, as do the people who come up with the ideas. There is even a list of people who have contributed multiple times, with the top person getting seven suggestions in eight quarters. Needless to say, that person has been promoted twice over the past two years.

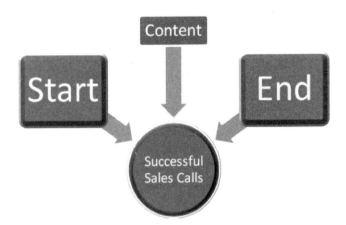

Figure 12-4. The start and end of a sales call.

NEXT-STEP MANAGEMENT

All sales organizations manage to revenue, but the really good ones manage to revenue *and* to a sales process; that is, they measure to "Give/Gets." Give/Gets are what you and the customer are giving to and getting from each other during each step of the sale, not on every call.

The idea of tracking what the sales team needs to accomplish at each step of a sales call needs to be a standard now. Deals are getting too complex and too loose. The sales teams, especially at the more senior levels, are tracking what the customers want them to do, rather than tracking what they should be doing. They should be asking, "What step are we at in the sales process? What is the revenue amount? What is being given to the prospect at this stage, and what are we asking for so they are giving something too?"

Along with revenue, percent of close, and close date, you may want to track Give/Gets. Great salespeople do this by always starting sales calls with the end in mind—that is, how they want the sales calls to end. If you track Give/Gets, you will be able to identify the mutual next step in a sale, because all parties are involved. In addition, if sales calls start and end with Give/Gets, then you can keep out of selling and get back into managing and coaching, which is your job, right?

Examples of Give/Gets are:

- Demos
- Proposals
- Education calls
- Financial discussions
- Relevant data
- Executive briefings
- Plant tours
- Trials

Intro to Boss - your

Make proposal to the dec. makers (ind. or team ?)

Get set up on terms
Sign the Scope of work.

Site Survey
Tour VCA's facility
get a tour of their facility

(Almost every sales call should be focused on the Give/Gets.) And for a management team in a real sales culture, this should be part of the forecast.

This is the normal conversation of a sales organization that is ProActive, not reactive. By tracking the Give/Gets, you can be assured your sales team is:

- ProActively asking the customer to participate, not just giving and giving to the prospect and being a part of a one-way relationship

- Making progress from the buyer's perspective, not just the seller's perspective

- Measuring what is going to go on at the beginning and the end of the sales call and the sales process, where control of the sales call is anyway

Be ProActive and track success at the beginning and the end of a sales call. Track Give/Gets.

MANAGEMENT OF THE SALES CALL
AND SALES TEAM

If your team wants to manage from both sides of the equation—not just from the selling side—you'll need to measure buyer activity rather than just the sales call or the sales process.

Management of the sales team requires the management team to get out of the day-to-day sale and get ahead of the game. Manage the sales process from the buyer's perspective, and you will help your team, your customer, and your company. Not bad, eh?

I'll Show Them
How to Do It

"Generals who lead their armies into battle are the most respected. But those are also the generals who get shot."

It is all made for TV. You know the war-movie scene, where the big battle is about to begin. Both sides are ready; the war will be won or lost with this upcoming, decisive battle. The generals from both armies get ready. Of course, each is on a white horse and in the most colorful outfit you can imagine. They give the motivational call to arms and then lead their troops into battle.

Of course, who do you think the other army is aiming for? Not the general's horse, that's for sure.

From a sales-management perspective, way too many sales organizations have their sales managers running around trying to close business. Why? Isn't that what the salesperson is trying to do? Oh, so the sales organization invents new terms:

- Team Selling

- Matrix Selling

- Overlay Selling

- Partner Selling

It gets quite confusing, and the more overlays, the more money it's going to cost the company to get a dollar of revenue.

> **"The problem is, sales management does not know what to do with their time!"**

Stop and think about this for a minute. It's a tough time, and the VP of sales is being called in by senior management to find out if the company is going to make its revenue targets. What happens next? The VP then calls the sales directors, the directors call the managers, and the managers call the salespeople. Okay, what are they all doing? Two things:

1.   Looking at the past

2.   Trying to predict what the salespeople should do

So what happens? The sales managers get involved and start helping the salespeople, who don't need the help. But the managers are going to help anyway because they:

- Know more

- Are the boss

- Can do what they want because they own the gold

Here's how the cycle works. The manager starts selling and starts getting the sales team dependent on him. The members of the sales team feel like the manager is with the troops, helping to close business, so the manager looks good and the company makes its number.

So you have managers selling, salespeople helping the managers, directors trying to keep score, and VPs looking at forecasts that are 60 percent accurate at best. The problem again is the generals . . . er, sales managers, who don't know what to do. The good generals know what to do.

Great generals, like great sales managers, are not getting deeper into the battle (or the sale, in this situation). They are planning the next battle—and the battle after that. They are getting their sales teams—troops—ready for the next three to six months.

The mistake companies make, especially in tough times, is to work harder

---

Where Do You Stay?

A friend of mine who is also in the sales and sales-management training business ranks his clients like hotels.

"I have some Ritz-Carltons, some Hiltons, some Holiday Inns, and some Motel 6 accounts. It is really easy to tell who is who and much harder to get the lower ones to act and perform like the higher ones.

What sets the lower hotels apart from the higher hotels is not what you think. It really does not have anything to do with the intelligence of the sales team or the market they are in per se. Mostly, it has to do with the commitment by the organization to learn. When we train, the managers are learning in the class too, and that makes a huge difference. We also offer the managers a follow-up session for free. And only the top 'hotels' take us up on the offer."

---

at closing business and getting the forecast to look better so that more deals close. Everyone pitches in and gets more business. That's great, but what are you going to replace it with?

Thus, there are three things great sales organizations do to stay ahead of the curve:

- Increase intelligence

- Increase performance

- Challenge the team

> **"Learning is a culture, not an event."**

LEARNING PRINCIPLES

Great sales organizations work at getting their sales teams smarter, and they have them work together so that the vision of the sales managers is in line with what the salespeople are doing. What are you doing to make your sales teams smarter?

Imagine George Washington getting ready for the battle at Valley Forge.

"Hey, I didn't even think it was going to be cold. I haven't trained my troops to fight in the snow, and heck, we don't even have warm clothes. When we planned this battle, it was a great fall day. Who knew? I was busy with the troops over at the gun-cleaning seminar."

There are five rules for making your teams smarter. As a general understanding, these are what the management team should be focusing on—not helping to close a sale.

1. **Rule #1: Predict the Future.** What is the market, the competition, the sales team going to need and do six months from now, and what are you doing to get ready for it?

2. **Rule #2: Get Involved.** If you are going to teach the sales team new skills, such as value selling, new products, new packaging, negotiation, or presentation skills, what is the management team doing to learn these skills well enough so it can coach and instill the new skills in the salespeople? There are many sales training programs in which the managers sit through a class. But because they are not selling, they forget these lessons and then go back to their subjective ways of management. They ask:

"How's the deal coming? When do you think we are going to get it?"

And they ask these things right after a training class! It's frustrating.

3. **Rule #3: Make It a Process.** Where is your sales process? When you make changes to it, are you changing and documenting the process? This is what sales managers should be working on, but because they have had no training in process management, they do not feel the need to work the process. Big mistake.

4. **Rule #4: Make the Best Better.** What are you doing to get your A players to A+ status? This should be well documented and worked at on a weekly basis. The best will set new standards and define new ideas to modify the current process, in addition to making their quotas.

I talked to a senior sales manager the other day and asked her to name her top two salespeople. I then asked members of her management team what it was doing to get these people to A+ status.

They thought about that for a while, like it was a trick question, and then said a couple of things. Then they looked for acknowledgment for at least doing something.

I then asked the top two salespeople what they thought they needed to do to elevate their games. They came up with two or three things that could be done easily, but that the sales managers had no idea about. Sell, sell, sell . . . is that the only answer?

5. **Rule #5: Overcome Fears.** It's fear that stops us from changing the way we do things. That fear of the unknown and fear of failure are pretty strong. More and more, we see managers holding their sales teams back, rather than the salespeople holding themselves back. The managers must have the faith, trust, and confidence in their salespeople, get out of the way, and focus on the next three to six months.

Stay focused on these five rules and you will be doing more for your sales team than you know. You will be doing the job that you thought you were doing. Now you know.

LEADERSHIP AND COACHING

I heard from many senior managers when I asked them about their mistakes in this specific area. How did they provide great leadership and coaching to the organization?

What I learned was that when coaching or leadership lets employees come up with their own ideas, that is a leverage play, and it is how organizations stay competitive. The two keys to this are the question-and-options-based coaching method and learning to look for the second right answer.

Question-and-Options-Based Coaching

When the customer talks and you listen, you get results. So why do sales managers feel the need to impart their wisdom to salespeople? Instead of telling them what to do in a given situation, ask them questions. After all, there is usually a question behind a question. If you do this and then have the employee list some options to solve his own problem, everyone wins. A question-and-options-based coaching style can also help with your planning efforts because you may learn a few things, as opposed to imparting that wisdom again. Figure 13-1 demonstrates this idea.

But look at Figure 13-2. If this is the model for great coaching and learning, how do you make sure the employee sees, hears, says, and does?

The answer is to role play. Bring in the video camera and have people practice their new presentations. Have salespeople double up with one another when they work a trade show. Find ways for them to gain experience without you there.

●————— **THE SECOND RIGHT ANSWER** ●———

Paradigms change, and it is up to sales management to have the sales team start thinking out of the box. Without this, salespeople will be doing the same things they did years ago, expecting the same results, even though the market and the buyers have changed. Not a good recipe for success.

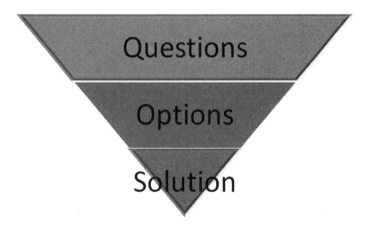

Figure 13-1. The question-and-options-based coaching model.

We remember

20% of what we read
30% of what we hear
40% of what we see
50% of what we say
60% of what we do
and
90% of what we see, hear, say, and do.

Figure 13-2. How easily we forget.

Dewitt Jones, a *National Geographic* photographer and a motivational speaker, says it this way:

"I am always looking for the second right answer.
If I stopped at the first right answer, life would be boring.
When I get to the place of a second right
answer, the answers just keep coming and coming."

What are you doing to keep your team looking for the second right answer? You need to keep challenging your team, and in addition, you need to get yourself out of the way. Here is an example of this in action. It's a story relayed to me by one of those great sales managers.

I have 250 salespeople in my organization, with four regional vice presidents and 28 regional managers, so about 300 people overall.

Our forecast accuracy had slipped to about 70 percent. We had come from 50 percent forecast accuracy a few years ago, and through a lot of pain and growth, we got it up to 90 percent on a 90-day rolling window. We were getting a lot of "maybes" in the funnel, and that is never any good.

We knew the way to get rid of maybes was with the Implementation Date, or I-Date. We started asking, "What date is the customer going to use what we sell?" instead of, "When are they going to sign our contract?" Salespeople, sales managers, and even the sales VPs know about I-Dates, so just reinforcing the tools we already knew and were familiar with was going to have limited success.

So we got seven or eight key individuals and asked them what the issue was. We got three major answers:

1. *The pricing for the new product was so different, customers did not understand it.*

2. *The sales team did not really understand all the variations of the new product.*

3. *Proposals were taking twice as long because the team had to be really careful with the new product quotes.*

Okay, so we knew what the issues were, and we were about to recommend that the marketing and sales departments come up with an answer—and soon. This is how we have always done it in the past, and though a bit cumbersome, it does work.

Then two of the regional vice presidents came up with a suggestion. How about if each regional manager presented an idea of how to solve this issue on his own, implemented that idea, and reported back within 60 days?

Well, this was a stupid idea. How could this possibly work? But, I thought about it. It really was their problem, and if they could come up with more than one right answer, this could have great benefits. Usually, marketing came up with an answer, and one or two of the regions had a huge headache about it. It took two months just to announce a workable solution, and not everyone would like it. Here was the potential for three solutions. Three right answers.

The danger was lack of a standard. But the risk was minimal because the VPs knew the goal was for each of them to get back to 90 percent forecast accuracy.

The result: Three of the VPs worked together, one worked by himself. Sixty days later, we had two solutions that made sense, we were back up to 88 percent forecast accuracy, and we were trending upward. Oh, and we had four very happy sales VPs.

Me? I spent my time on the end-of-the-year issues (90 days ahead of actuals) and we ended up having a great year. All because I believed in letting the team look for more than one right answer.

I'm Superman

*"The more hours in the day I spend on the job,
the more successful I will become."*

Imagine what it will take for you to become successful in your next job. Spend some time during the week and pretend that you already have the job. What would you be doing? What would you be doing differently?

> *Workaholic Manager:* One who works 50 to 80 hours per week and expects the rest of the sales management team, as well as the sales team, to do the same.
>
> *Superman:* See Workaholic Manager above.
>
> *ProActive Manager:* One who delegates and manages forward and upward.

Yes, you do incredible things. You manage a sales organization, you work long hours, you are successful, but are you really ready for the next level?

A senior manager told me recently about his philosophy on sales managers and promotions. He told his managers that if they wanted to get promoted, they had to stop working so hard at what they did every day. The hamster on a treadmill, running-faster theory applies to managers too.

Success is not a matter of how hard you work. It is a matter of perspective. When you detach from your current environment, you have a tendency to become more productive. This would be the forest-from-the-trees syndrome, so to speak.

Your job is to execute the company's and your boss's plans and strategies. You are not an entrepreneur. You are the revenue arm of the company, not an outsourced resource. Way too many managers admit to not keeping this perspective in mind when making decisions about their sales teams.

On the other hand, and it is a big other hand, way too many sales managers admit they do exactly what their companies ask of them. They do all the paperwork, file all the call reports, input all the data in the CRM/SFA system, and they miss their numbers. That is a mistake too. So what is the answer to that inevitable question:

How do I work smarter, not harder?

Here are some of the things some sales managers are doing now instead of working harder: Train, Measure, and Communicate.

● TRAIN ●

As a manager, you are always looking to give your sales team a competitive edge. You invest in training DVDs, podcasts, courses, and motivational speakers at the annual meeting to make sure your team is razor sharp. But here's a question: What are you doing for you?

A common mistake sales managers make is not getting any training. Oh sure, first-line sales managers go (usually they're sent) to sales-management courses. A year or two later they go to a "Sales Management II" course, but then that's it.

Forty hours a year. That's the minimum amount of training you should get, and you need to schedule it or it will never get done. Where can you go?

- Organizations that offer public seminars
- Local universities

- Noted universities like Stanford, Harvard, Northwestern, and UCLA

- Night schools or extension programs that offer MBA programs

- Google or Yahoo! (search for training programs)

- *The Selling Power* Sales Leadership Conference or a conference sponsored by *Sales and Marketing Management* magazine

Take courses on time management, new software tools, Web services, management coaching, and communication skills. It is not about getting smarter, it is about working smarter with more tools in your tool shed. The average sales manager completes fewer than 16 hours of training in a year. That's a two-day program once a year. Do it for your team, the company, yourself, and your network. You will be amazed at how well your network expands by attending one of these events. Do it for all of these reasons.

Heck, take your boss or peers to one. You never know what will happen when you get them smarter too.

● MEASURE ●

Because you are not being Superman or Superwoman, you can now set some metrics with your boss. Besides revenue goals, ask your boss what is important to the organization. The topics will center on a 3×3 matrix. This 3×3 action plan (see Figure 14-1) is something you want to keep by your side. It reminds you what is important, what you need to stay focused on the day to day, and

Action Plan Q1	Past	Present	Future
Down			
Across			
Up			

Figure 14-1. The 3×3 Action Plan, ready for Q1.

acts as your own report card for you to see how far you have come up the ladder—and how far you still have to go.

The 3×3 is a working document that allows you to keep a finger on what is important in all directions. It gives you all *perspectives* in all *time zones*. It allows you to be ProActive and put the what-do-we-need-to-be-better syndrome in your control.

Perspectives

The 3×3 has three perspectives: down, across, and up.

> The "Down" perspective is about what you are going to do for your organization or direct reports. It allows you to stay focused on that one thing you need to do for your team. It reminds you to stay the course and not get distracted by the day-to-day fires.
>
> The "Across" perspective is about things you and a peer can do together or things a colleague would like to do with you.
>
> The "Up" perspective addresses things you can do for or with a boss. This does not necessarily mean *your* boss, just someone of higher rank.

Why do this? Why commit to things that cross boundaries? Do it because the manager who has effective communication skills always comes out ahead. The manager who likes to play it close to the vest and does not want to share information is seen as secretive, scheming, and therefore not as trustworthy as one who openly communicates.

Time Zones

Metrics need to be spread over time, and your organization works in different time zones. If you want to be on top of your game, you have to look across time to be effective. This means considering the past, present, and future.

Past. Commit to solving a problem—something that happened in the past and needs work. This might include:

- A CRM/SFA system that is not working well

- A sales process that is out of date

- A commission plan that is not working well

These are items that need to be fixed, and managers have a tendency to gravitate to these first and often.

Present. Address things that are happening today too; opportunities such as:

- A contest to get a new product selling faster

- An end-of-quarter contest

- An important deal that will have an effect on the company in an unusual way

There are many tasks and duties that can fit into this category, and therefore managers seem to spend most of their time here. To be effective, only pick the ones that would be important to your boss or senior management, not the ones that are just important to you.

Future. This area is for the items that are going to affect the future, or tasks that you will deal with in the coming three to six months, such as:

- Next year's compensation plan

- A new territory you are going to be opening up

- Imminent headcount situations and redeployments

Your bosses will have the most interest in the future, and you will have the least amount of detail about it. This is good because great managers want to get others involved in their plans.

COMMUNICATION CHANNELS

Finally, a word about communication channels is relevant when talking about doing too much.

In the Internet age, where speed is king, most people are not working on content or quality. It seems it is more important to "get it out there" than to take some time and think about what to say. Likewise, managers say they are forced into speed situations. In my research, managers said they would like to have taken some more time on almost 50 percent of their decisions. They noted that when they sent a message or informed people of a decision, the message was often incomplete and not well thought out. <u>In most cases, speed should not be the first driver of management.</u>

> *I held a two-day planning meeting with 11 of my direct reports. On day one, there was a lot of material, a lot of speed, and a lot of distractions. Blackberrys were going off, laptops were open, and people were coming in and out of the meeting because of e-mails and voice mails. It just seemed really hectic and chaotic.*
>
> *On day two, we made it a rule not to open laptops, and we turned off our cell phones. There were no outside distractions. It was a great, productive day. We got so much accomplished that we finished ahead of schedule!*
>
> *Could we make sure laptops and cell phones are off at every meeting? I really don't know, but at least half of the time we're going to follow this rule. Everyone's involvement is much higher and the decisions seem to come faster. Go figure.*

PART FOUR

INFRASTRUCTURE DECISIONS

"I have learned throughout my life as a composer chiefly through my mistakes and pursuits of false assumptions, not by my exposure to founts of wisdom and knowledge."
—Igor Stravinsky (1882–1971)

Time to look at how you're managing your own shop—that is, your infrastructure. It's time for a checkup, a tuneup, a spring cleaning.

The biggest infrastructure mistakes managers reported in our research fall into two buckets:

1. "I did not adapt to change fast enough. I thought I knew what to do; I figured the way we did it before would work again."

2. "I was not strict enough. I let it go on for too long. I knew it was getting out of hand, I was too loose, had too many other more important fires. I was not getting the results we needed, but I thought it would turn around."

Looking at your own organization is hard. When you get a new job or a new promotion, all you really have are the first 90 days to make any true changes. After that, your view starts to get clouded by the rest of the organization. You get too close and cannot tell the forest from the trees as easily as you did during those first few months.

So chapters 15 through 20 are about the top mistakes managers told me they wished they could have avoided in running their organizations, and what they did about them.

It's Their Territory

"It's the company's territory; salespeople are just renting it. Because they are the renters, they should be given the latitude to decorate it the way they want."

This is an interesting analogy, and in many cases, managers believe that sales is an art and a science.

The amount of freedom you give a salesperson is directly related to that person's success. The more success salespeople have, the more freedom they get. The inverse is also true. The less success they have, the more instruction or help they get. So what are some of the ways sales management should look at territories so the company gets the maximum benefit and the maximum revenue?

"One of the biggest mistakes I ever made was letting the salespeople decide territories. They came to me with what made sense, and they did quite a bit of homework. I was blinded and did not really want to take on the project, so I approved it. Not a good idea. Three months later, half the team was complaining that the territories were not fair, and they were lied to by the other half."

OPTIMUM SALES TERRITORIES

The question most managers ask is: what is optimum? What is the best way to maximize revenue, minimize expenses, and keep everyone happy and motivated? Well, there are three keys to territory management that will let you feel you have maximized the situation.

- Division
- Time
- Rewards

These three topics will define the culture you want to set. Culture is a lot about your actions, not your intent, so if you can decide on what you want to do with these three areas, you will have gone a long way toward maximizing the opportunities and setting your culture.

THREE WAYS TO DIVIDE TERRITORIES

There are three ways to divide a territory up:

- By geography
- By product
- By customer

Geography

Geographic territory division is the easiest way to divide up a sales territory. This is where you measure out some geographic area, like Europe or the Pacific Northwest, and then divide it up among resources. The advantages are that the method is easy to apply, boundaries are already defined, and usually you can adjust resources based on where the salespeople are located. Territory disputes can be handled by customer ZIP or postal codes.

There are some disadvantages too. Cross-territory customers and potential multiple-product salespeople per territory might exist, for example.

Product

Product territory division is a good idea for an inbound or e-based sales team. This is where salespeople are divided up by product line and can also be divided up by major accounts within that product line.

For example, consider a plastics manufacturer that sells many products. Some are automotive. The salesperson, who had the automotive products to sell, would also have the auto companies as major accounts for all products. The advantage of having both types of product-based territories is a high degree of specialization and motivation. The disadvantages are the potential for multiple salespeople calling on one customer and a sales team that is not focused on customer solutions.

Customer

Territories that are divided up by customer are usually called "account-based" territories. Sometimes these territories are classified, usually by Standard Industrial Classification (SIC) codes. The big advantage is that salespeople have a high degree of customer knowledge. The disadvantage is that this type of territory assignment does not generally promote a high degree of prospecting. Salespeople usually stay focused on the top half of the prospect food chain.

Many organizations have a mix of territories, but the rules are the same. What is right for you? That depends on the sales objectives. The truth is, most managers stay with their territory schemes too long, when they should have shaken them up earlier. So shake up the territory and compensation plan every three years. The benefits of this action far outweigh the "sit on your hands, everything is good" mentality. Be ProActive.

────● TIME: SUBANNUAL TERRITORIES ●────

Who made the law that territories are good for a year? That was before the Internet age and the speed of customer demands. Many sales organizations are going to semiannual or quarterly territory assignments.

The smaller the average sales price and the shorter the sales cycle, the more this is an option for many teams. Larger sales prices and long sales cycles do not really lend themselves well here.

With that caveat stated, modifying territories and compensation on a semiannual or quarterly basis has its advantages.

- It provides a fresh approach every time a change is made.

- The company is not as dependent on a single salesperson's competency in a territory.

- It increases prospecting skills.

- It produces fewer complaints about how the salesperson has tried and cannot get through to the right person, the right buyer, etc.

Managers claim they shake up entire territories this way, but most have a territory *modifier* approach. For example, say a company has 100 salespeople, each with a list of 25 accounts. At the end of a quarter, each salesperson should have added to that list of accounts based on new business with new customers. So the average salesperson at the end of a quarter has, say, 29 accounts, which is four too many. The salesperson has to select four accounts to drop or turn into house accounts so the starting number for the next quarter is back at 25. The house accounts are then allocated to the inside sales team or to new salespeople coming on board.

This system works well for the company that is trying to get new-name accounts and/or penetrate accounts broadly and deeply. Because salespeople do not want to give up accounts, they will spend more time making this system work. If that's the case, this approach often works well.

● REWARDS DEFINED ●

Just as compensation is doled out for revenue, you should also look at rewards for territory management. Here are some ideas.

Drive the Business, not the Territory

Management needs to do its homework and look at the business, not just the territories. Way too often you hear sales managers say things like, "Gail has the Southeast territory. She did $4.5 million last year. She could probably do $5 million next year."

That's great for Gail, but what can the *territory* do? What is the business expectation for the Southeast? If the competition is growing at 50 percent, shooting for 11 percent growth is not really a good business move. Companies have access to quite a bit of information that will tell sales management what

---

The Right Territories?

We had five geographic territories to work with when it came time to assign quotas. So, at the beginning of the next year, instead of the usual 8 to 12 percent increase, we looked at what was going on in the territory for our industry.

We came to find out that our worst-performing territory was growing the fastest, and our best territory, in terms of growth, total revenue, and industry standards, was performing the worst.

We determined that we had our best manager in the worst-performing territory, but we thought our second-best manager was in the "best" territory.

Instead of replacing the manager in the best territory, we showed him the data we had compiled, and after he understood the ramifications, he got mad. He was upset that he was not driving his team to be the best it could be, especially given his quota increase that year. He thought his team was doing the best it could.

Here's the bottom line: The best territory grew 42 percent. Once the managers got out of their own way, they realized they could perform past what they were doing. They were holding themselves back.

We let the data define the territories and quotas, not the usual management-planning sessions that turn into nothing but shouting matches. We now believe we are maximizing the business, not just the territory.

---

economic conditions prevail by region, by sector, and by SIC. Winging it is what people do with sales calls, not with territory management. Maximize the revenue, don't allocate territories.

So ask yourself these four questions.

1. What is the market in the territory now? How much of our stuff and competitors' stuff is being purchased?

2. What major accounts do our competitors have in the territory?

3. What are the growth expectations by product, SIC, and customer?

4. What is fueling the growth? If you sell air conditioning units and plan on 10 percent growth in a normal market, but new home sales are up by 50 percent, watch out! You are going to have a great ("sandbag") year.

Positive and Negative Rewards

Salesperson A, who maximizes her sales plan based on territory optimization, should be better compensated than salesperson B, who has a great territory  that grew less than the market did, even if salesperson B sold more dollars than salesperson A. Reward the effort and achievement of someone who can maximize a territory, then reward the person with more compensation and even more territory!

These rewards might include:

- Bonuses
- Recognition
- Acknowledgment
- More territory
- Promotion

On the other hand, although I don't recommend using negative rewards to manage long-term growth, they are effective for getting someone's attention. Negative rewards for inaction or misrepresentation might include:

- Taking away accounts
- Reassigning territory
- Redistributing territory assets
- Creating a lower commission structure for certain accounts/products

Examples of negative rewards come easy, don't they? They shouldn't, but they do. The use of negative rewards, when it comes down to it, will affect short-term behavior. But moderate or heavy use will be detrimental in the long run and is not recommended.

It's the *company's* territory. How you manage it is up to you. Sure, you would like a salesperson to take some pride of ownership and work it like it is his own, but in the final analysis, it is your responsibility to maximize territories.

The topic of territory maximization is a sneaky one. Managers may believe they are maximizing their sales resources based on constraints such as the salespeople's experience, where they are located, and other factors. However, in our research, the consensus is that when managers started looking at territory maximization rather than quota maximization, two things became apparent:

1. They have been leaving money on the table.

2. They have been listening to the B and C players whine instead of looking objectively at their responsibilities.

The sales managers we have spoken with believe they were leaving 10 to 15 percent of their revenues out in the territory because they assigned territory based on their resources rather than based on an objective look at what is out there.

The ability to maximize resources is a never-ending struggle. It is not easy to get rid of bad performers, let alone marginal ones. Being ProActive and planning for the territory juggling act should be part of your day-to-day job so you do not end up getting backed into a corner. Successful managers will tell you that territories are in management's realm, not the salesperson's.

I Have a Sales Process . . . I Think

"It's all about connecting the dots, following a game plan, reading the score. So without a well-defined sales process, guess what sales managers are doing?"

Without a well-defined sales process, sales managers aren't doing much. They are not leveraging assets. They are letting the salespeople create their own best practices.

Without leverage, you are not doing your job. Sales process, for the managers who were surveyed, was a top-three issue for the ones who had a process. And they regretted not implementing one sooner.

On the other hand, managers interviewed who had no sales process—or thought they had one, but it was "not well documented or followed"—thought the lack of a sales process was not that big of a deal.

So under the category of "You don't know what you are missing unless you have a working one," here are the mistakes sales managers often make regarding the sales process.

WHAT IS A SALES PROCESS?

Is this a good question or what? Here are some actual answers from managers who do not understand what a sales process can do.

> "We don't really have one. We sort of have one."
>
> "We have a great process. It's not really followed too well, but we have the process down."
>
> "If we tie the salesperson's hands with a sales process, sales will take longer."

Sales managers usually abhor sales processes for two reasons. First, they didn't like following a process when they were selling, so why should anyone else? Second, they are managing to revenue, so why do they need to follow a process? After all, when you are managing to revenue, you are managing reactively. And if all you are ever going to do is track to the final score—not *how* you got to the final score—then a sales process really doesn't matter after all, right?

It *matters.*

WHAT DOESN'T WORK

When discussing sales process, the list of what doesn't work is long. In fact, it can cover more than a few books. When asked about what they have tried that did not work, there seems to be a general consensus among sales managers:

- Winging it; that is, letting each salesperson sell on his own

- Having a 10-slide PowerPoint deck describing what your sales process is so everyone can understand it

- A "Here Is Our Sales Process" memo

- Convincing themselves that they do not need one or that they have one already (also called *denial*)

- Going with the canned sales process in their CRM systems

- Copping one from a friend

The list could go on and on. It's true that if you have a sales process that doesn't work, at least you can fix it. Where it gets really difficult is when you have a process that management put into place, spent quite a bit of time on, and feels good about, but that the salespeople do not even bother to use. Here comes that denial again.

Managers must implement a sales process that first-line managers accept, have had a part in developing, and will use in their day-to-day coaching. Without the first-line managers' buy-in—*not the salespeople's but the first-line sales managers'*—it just won't work.

● WHAT WORKS ●

Probably less than 30 percent of all companies have a sales process that works. That said, those 30 percent are in the top 10 percent of sales efficiency, sales-cycle control, and ability to go broad and deep in an account.

Follow this five-step process and you will have the makings of a sales process.

1. Define the buyer's process.

2. Determine what needs to be accomplished in each step of that process.

3. Determine what the salespeople need to do in each step.

4. Determine which tools the salespeople can use.

5. Determine what salespeople can give and get from the customer at each step.

What really works is capturing your sales process and managing to it. For example, look at the sales process in Figure 16-1. This one is fictitious because most companies treat their sales processes as a competitive advantage. This could be modified though for almost any company, and it has been many times.

Sales Step	Objectives	Activities	Tools	Homework Give/Gets
Initiate	• Contact High in Organization • Start Qualification Process • Find a Dragon • Determine Next Step	Prospecting Process Lead Generation References Contacted	• 30 Second Speech • 20 Second Speech • PowerHour • Summarize/Bridge/Pull	Welcome Page *Initial Reasons* *Funding* *Competitive Landscape*
Educate	• Two Way Education • Top Two Competitive Features • Reason to Make Decision • Top Two Problems	Presentation #1 Discuss with All Levels for Needs Find Drivers Get Requirements for Demonstration	• TimeZones • Solution Box • Value Questions • Ask/Tell/Ask • 3 Languages • ValueStar	Input for Presentation Customer Success Document *Problem Page* *Org Chart* *Buy Process Document*
Value	• Mutual Qualification • I-Date with Dragons • Buy Process	Mutual Timeframes ROI Agreed To Roadmap Complete	• Money • Method • Motivation • I-Date • Trip-Tik	Trip-Tik Outline *Top Two Benefits* *Decision Path* *Executive Reason Statement*
Validate	• Transfer of Ownership • Plan to Implement • Solution Conformed • Meet with All Senior Contacts	Executive Demonstration Final User Demonstration Finalize Mutual Interest	• Ask/Tell/Ask • CliffDive • Yes • BOSS V • Value Tree	Decision Path Update *Dragons* *Trip-Tik Update*
Justify	• Final ROI • Final Mutual Proposal • Implementation Plan	Implementation Plan Terms and Conditions Finalized Submit Proposal	• ROI • I-Plan • 2 Wins	Final Proposal Reasons *Success Path* *Final ROI* *I-Plan Complete*
Decision	• Final Decision Made • First 30 Days Identified	Contract Executed Hand Off to Customer Support	• I-Plan • Negotiation Tools	Contract Thank You Letter *Contract Complete* *Relationship Contract*
Follow Thru	• Ensure Expectations are Identified	Ensure Order Processes Final Executive Discussion	• Customer Support Hand • Off Tool	Hand Off Tool

Figure 16-1. An example of a buy/sales process in the making.

Many companies have multiple processes for their different sales groups. Some may have a normal sales process and a major-account sales process. Some have multiple sales processes grouped by major product lines. More than three per company is way too many; 80 percent of companies have just one.

The five steps to create a sales process are not complicated. But it is surprising how many companies do not have an identified process or simply do not feel the need to have one. Sales forecasting is one part of the process, but as you can imagine, sales forecasting is the art of reactive prediction, not about identifying all the steps involved in buying and selling.

Forecasting is like telling your spouse when you are going to buy that new car and how much you are going to pay for it. What you say has nothing to do with how you make your decision. Similarly, forecasting has nothing to do with the Buying/Selection process either.

ProActive Sales Management has an identified buy/sales process. Coupled with the customer's timeline and budget, it is a tool with which salespeople and managers succeed. Figure 16.1 provides an example.

> The Buy/Sales process succeeds or fails in companies based on its acceptance and use by the first- and second-line managers. If these managers use the process, it will be a success. If they don't, the process is doomed to fail because the salespeople will be allowed to do whatever they want to do.

How can you develop a process that works for your organization? Follow the five steps and you are there. Let's take a closer look at each step.

STEP 1: DEFINE THE BUYER'S PROCESS

Typical buyers go through steps in their *buying process*. Typically, these are the components of that process:

1. **Initiate**. The buyer has a problem and motivation to do something about it.

2. *Educate*. The buyer learns what is available to meet her needs. This evaluation comes in all sizes and shapes, and there may be many ways to solve the problem, not just to buy from you.

3. *Value*. This is when mutual value is quantified. It's the hardest step for salespeople because the customer, not the salesperson, determines what *value* means.

4. *Validate*. This is where the transfer of ownership takes place. The buyer validates the match between need and solution.

5. *Justify*. This is the last step in the buying process before a decision is made. This is where buyer's remorse shows up; it's also when a prospect "goes dark."

6. *Decide*. This is the final step in a purchase decision.

7. *Follow Through*. This is when the salesperson hands the client to Customer Service/Installation.

This is a typical seven-step model. Buyers might use seven steps, four steps, nine steps—it really does not matter, although once you go past seven or so, it gets a bit complex. Figure 16-2 illustrates the steps.

You may have noticed that a buyer does not go through a qualification step. Buyers do not qualify themselves; that's what salespeople do. That's why Qualifying should never be used during the sales process as a step. It's something you have your team do every step of the way.

STEP 2: DETERMINE WHAT NEEDS TO BE ACCOMPLISHED IN EACH STEP OF THAT PROCESS

Without goals or specific tasks—*objectives*—salespeople are left to react to the buyer's whims. The old sales adage is so true:

Buyers want to be led.

The more the sales team takes control of the Buy/Sales process—that is, the more they learn how to control a sale—the better off they will be. You can have your team be ProActive and identify each step of the Buy/Sell process, as well as what needs to get accomplished.

Figure 16-2. Sales steps.

Now, is this a hard-and-fast rule? Don't you wish there were hard-and-fast rules in sales? No, each goal does not have to be met, but most salespeople will skip steps or components of steps because they're too hard, the salespeople are nervous, or they fear they may be doing the wrong thing. They figure that as long as they are doing what the customers ask of them, how can they be doing the wrong thing?

Yep, this is why you should document what needs to get accomplished at every step of the way, what has to be accomplished in order to feel successful at every stage, not just the end. Figure 16-3 is an example of these objectives.

No Justification, No Buy

A friend of mine just purchased one of the latest, biggest, hang-on-the-wall TVs you can buy.

He remodeled a room, so in this new room, he needed a TV (Initiate).

He went to the Web, talked to friends, and visited a few places that sold the TVs (Educate).

He measured the height and width, figured out where it would go, which type to buy, and how it would look. He also learned how to get it installed (Validate).

It was all set; he made the purchase and got the TV home. End of story . . . or sort of.

Now he went over his finances and figured out that the TV, the speakers, the receiver, the DVD player, the installation, and all the rest cost three times his initial budget. For what the room was going to be used for, he could not justify the expense. So back went the TV, and he had a heck of a time getting all his money back without a restocking fee.

All steps need to be documented in a buy process. You never know from the buyer's perspective what will make the sale or will cause it to come apart at the last minute.

If you have the process down, you can identify good and bad things before they happen, so you can have a ProActive sales team.

STEP 3: DETERMINE WHAT THE SALESPEOPLE NEED TO DO IN EACH STEP

Now it is time for the *activities*. What typically happens at each stage? What are some best practices other salespeople are following that others could mimic? This is the area where managers can do the most coaching. Instead of the usual "Listen to the salesperson and make comments," you now have an organization that can be ProActive and can coach to what needs to be done, rather than comment on what has already been done.

Activities usually are action items by both parties (see Figure 16-4). Typically, because the salesperson should be controlling the sales process, most of the items in this area will be activities the selling organization has

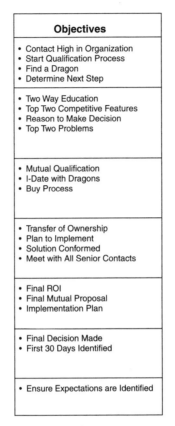

Figure 16-3. An example of sales objectives.

to accomplish. Because each buying organization is different, there needs to be room to allow for buyer input at every step. However, creating a list of these activities will help keep both parties on track.

STEP 4: DETERMINE WHICH TOOLS THE SALESPEOPLE CAN USE

This again is a very coachable area for the sales manager. A sales tool is a "Neutral Element." Each party, the salesperson, and the sales manger should

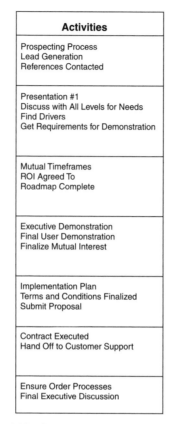

Figure 16-4. A sample activities list.

have an equal say in the use of the tool. The tool is neutral; it's just a tool. Both parties should be able to discuss how to use the tool, but under no circumstance does the sales tool become the sales manager's way of doing things. Tools like the ones in Figure 16-5 can show what needs to happen, but they should not take the place of good sales coaching.

Nor should it replace bad behavior with other bad behavior. A tool should be discussed when you are trying to conduct activities, not when you're just using the tool to use the tool.

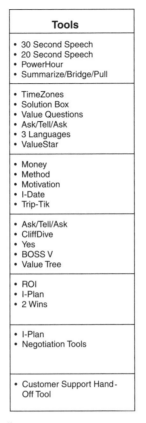

Tools
• 30 Second Speech • 20 Second Speech • PowerHour • Summarize/Bridge/Pull
• TimeZones • Solution Box • Value Questions • Ask/Tell/Ask • 3 Languages • ValueStar
• Money • Method • Motivation • I-Date • Trip-Tik
• Ask/Tell/Ask • CliffDive • Yes • BOSS V • Value Tree
• ROI • I-Plan • 2 Wins
• I-Plan • Negotiation Tools
• Customer Support Hand-Off Tool

Figure 16-5. A sample tools list.

STEP 5: DETERMINE WHAT SALESPEOPLE CAN GIVE AND GET FROM THE CUSTOMER AT EACH STEP

Give/Gets are set up to make sure salespeople do not give the farm away and confuse that for selling. Anybody can give stuff away; the art is having the customer see the value.

Gets from the prospect can be at the user level or the executive level, depending on what is needed during the sale. For example, during the Educate stage, the salesperson may want to be educated by the buyer on how the widget the salesperson is selling will be used. Or the salesperson may want to ask the prospect's senior managers for the return on investment (ROI)—an explanation of how what you are selling them will make them money.

Think of the Give/Gets as a fair way to negotiate a sale. If you are willing to put some resources into the process at every step, so should the prospect. Make sense? Figure 16-6 shows an example.

In most cases, salespeople are afraid to ask, or the buyer has laid out how they plan to proceed, and your sales team feels it must follow. Neither case is a good scenario, but they happen way too often.

A sales process creates a leverage that great sales managers use daily. The huge mistake sales managers often make is fooling themselves by thinking

---

Homework Give/Gets

Welcome Page
Initial Reasons
Funding
Competitive Landscape

Input for Presentation
Customer Success Document
Problem Page
Org Chart
Buy Process Document

Trip-Tik Outline
Top Two Benefits
Decision Path
Executive Reason Statement

Decision Path Update
Dragons
Trip-Tik Update

Final Proposal Reasons
Success Path
Final ROI
I-Plan Complete

Contract
Thank You Letter
Contract Complete
Relationship Contract

Hand Off Tool

Figure 16-6. A sample Give/Gets list.

they have a process somewhere within their organization. But the truth is, great sales processes are:

- Well documented
- Used by the salespeople
- Tracked by the sales managers
- Applied during coaching sessions
- Updated regularly
- Kept in the forefront of the sales team's actions

Managers have told me they are 20 to 40 percent more productive when their teams use sales processes. It's a mistake to leave that amount of revenue on the table. The golden rule about sales processes is:

IT'S ABOUT SPEED

Remember the slogan Bill Clinton used quite a bit in his first run for the office of President of the United States? "It's the economy, stupid."

It put political consultant James Carville on the map and Mr. Clinton in the White House. The same can be said for sales-process management. Well, *almost* the same—I would say, "It's the speed, stupid."

In other words, although completing every step is important, what's really at the heart of a good sales process is the speed in between each step.

Figure 16-7 is an example of a funnel. Each part is marked by what normally occurs at that stage of the sales process. In this example, a typical sale takes 31 days from start to finish. Using this data, the manager has the ability to manage each stage rather than manage the whole sale.

The comment we have heard most often from managers after they see how this funnel works is,

"What have I been *doing?!*"

The insight and ProActive sales-management action that can be taken by the sales-management team can be measured. It's one thing to measure funnel accuracy, funnel loads, and the size and shape of the funnel. Measuring speed is something else.

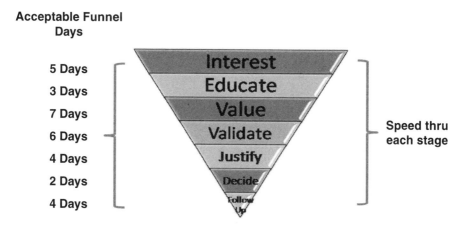

Figure 16-7. The funnel.

How does this tie into customer relationship management (CRM)/ sales force automation (SFA) systems?

Most SFA and CRM systems allow for working with a funnel and some degree of funnel management. These dashboards or detailed account-management tools have been around for quite some time, and using them should be a high priority for you and your organization.

It should be stressed that all these automation systems do is automate. If you have a bad sales process—or one that is poorly documented—all automation will do is, well, automate your bad practices.

It's better to change your process and then to automate that.

Metrics and Dashboards Are for Rookies

"Seat-of-the-pants managers need to realize we are not in the Stone Age any more. Welcome to metrics 2.0."

I manage to metrics. I track enough to choke a horse. My team tracks the number of sales calls, number of presentations, the ratio of presentations to demonstrations, the ratio of demonstrations to closed business, dollar volumes, margins, sales calls to revenue, and the total increase from the previous month, previous year, and year to date. What am I missing?

———————————● **METRICS IS THE JOB** ●———————————

How you are measuring the performance of the sales team is just as important as what you are measuring. Since the beginning of time, management has placed heavy emphasis on:

- **The Past:** What a salesperson or sales team has done in the past month, six months, whatever, as a prediction of the future.

- *Digital Photos:* Also called Snapshot Management, this is where management uses data from a single point in time, such as the end of a quarter or the first week of the month. While valuable, it does nothing to suggest how to make things better or how to continue the performance causing overachievement.

Measurement is the job of sales management, but too many sales managers feel their job is to sell. Funny, that's what you have salespeople for. Be they first-line, second-line, or senior management:

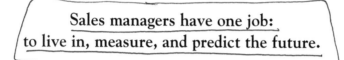

Sales managers have one job:
to live in, measure, and predict the future.

It's the movie, not the snapshot.

So the question is: What are the key metrics?

Again, asking this question of sales managers who have attended the school of hard knocks brings some insight. What not to measure is almost as important as what *to* measure, and you need to measure the video, not the picture. How? By measuring the gaps.

Gap Management is an important part of individual performance. Now you want to use the same principle you used in Gap Plans to measure the performance of your sales team and individual contributors.

Dashboard Options: Gap Management

What's important? What needs to get done? Assess what is really important over the next three to six months and then measure that. As shown in Figure 17-1, you will be measuring actual performance to a goal, over time, with a view of the future as well.

A few examples are in order.

Example #1: Prospecting for New Business Calls Per Week

Let's take the example of Darla and Jim. Darla has managed Jim for three years, and Jim has done well, always in the top 20 percent of the sales team. Recently, Jim has focused on his current customer base to get revenue, which

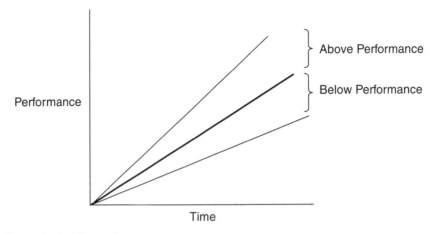

Figure 17-1. The performance gap.

is great. But his territory has quite a few new prospects in it since a major competitor closed its doors a few months back. Darla and Jim have a meeting in which Jim agrees that $200,000 of new business is out there for him to take. To achieve that goal, Jim will have to close four new accounts.

Darla and Jim agree that for the next quarter Jim needs to have three face-to-face meetings with new prospects every week so that at the end of the quarter, he will have made 35 new prospecting calls. The Gap Chart for this plan is in Figure 17-2.

To get to the goal of 35 by the end of the quarter, Jim has agreed to make three calls per week. Overachievement is 40, and minimum performance is 30. Now Darla and Jim can track weekly performance. So after four weeks, Jim's chart looks like Figure 17-3.

Now, Jim has good intentions, but his performance is not in line with the agreement. Darla can see it, Jim can see it, and a solution must be put into place before it is too late.

The Gap Chart in this situation:

- Made the performance issue visual

- Did not allow it to go to the back burner

- Allowed Jim to track himself and correct himself

- Gave Darla the opportunity to do her job rather than stay on Jim about this issue

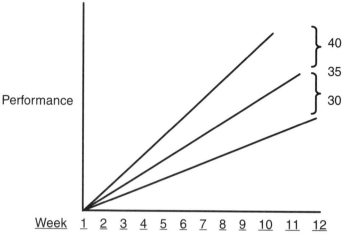

Figure 17-2. Darla and Jim's Gap Chart.

This is a simple example. Let's look at a team example.

Example #2: Revenue from New Customers Per Month

Darla has positioned her team to take advantage of the new business opportunity afforded them by the loss of a competitor. She is going to measure new

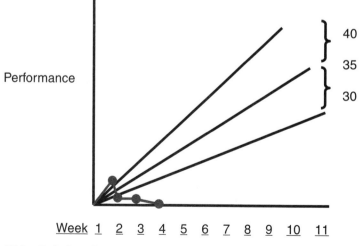

Figure 17-3. Jim's Gap Chart.

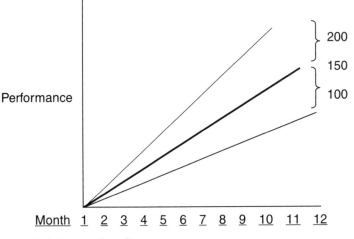

Figure 17-4. Darla's team Gap Chart.

business from new customers on a monthly basis. For this to happen, Darla will track the number of presentations to vice presidents and above on a monthly basis over the course of the year. Her Gap Chart looks like the one in Figure 17.4.

The first-quarter results for the team are in Figure 17-5.

The mistake most sales managers make is putting a binary goal out there—something such as: *We make it or do not make it. Yes or no. All or nothing.* But by using Gap Charts, the benefits of the overachievement and underachievement goals are obvious. The team can track what it can do something about: making presentations. Tracking revenue is important, but it does not tell the sales team specifically what to do. It's like telling a band to play your favorite song but not telling them what you think, specifically, makes the song great.

Gap Charts can augment the dashboard and should be seen as a way to get the sales team to the revenue goal. They focus on the future—what needs to be done. And they show progress like a video instead of like a snapshot.

Along that same theme, you should note that annual metrics are dead. The annual quota, annual compensation, and annual performance review are all dinosaurs. Quarterly and monthly metrics have taken the place of annual reviews. Why? Time.

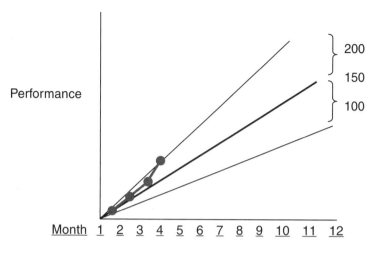

Figure 17-5. The team's Gap Chart.

HOW DID I GET 10 MONTHS TO MAKE A 12-MONTH NUMBER?

The typical sales manager allows deals to slip, which then shortens the amount of time a sales team has to close business. Let's say Gail has a deal she is going to close in March, and it slips until May. Instead of doing everything she can to close this piece of business in March, if Gail is on an annual quota, she is not that broken up by the deal slipping until May. Heck, she'll be happy to take the deal and run. There are, however, two mistakes with this thinking.

1. Although she is closing March business in May, by December, she will be closing October business and run out of time to close November and December business in the calendar year.

2. In addition, this type of delay thinking in March will cause a logjam or "hockey stick" of business by the end of the year, which Gail and her boss will rationalize by saying something like, "Well, it's just the nature of the business." After a year or so, Gail and her boss will lose their jobs because they couldn't get all that "hockey stick" business in time to make the number.

It just takes too long to turn a battleship. The market demands nimbler, quicker decisions and faster reactions. Gap Charts will help you get to that ultimate destination.

● "KING" OF METRICS ●

Besides revenue, what did you want to talk to me about?
—FAMOUS SALES MANAGER QUOTE

Revenues is the end game. But you have to play the whole game

It's all about revenue. The final measure. When it all comes down to it, you have to look at the revenues. That's the endgame, and no matter how well you played, they look at the score at the end of the game.

If you want to win these games, you have to put yourself in the position to win. That means doing the right things all the time. You cannot just play the final minute; you have to play the whole game. If this is true, then you need to measure the whole game.

Managers make a huge mistake by only looking at revenue on their dashboards. They should look at the items that *cause* revenue to happen. There are three: Frequency, Competency, and Time, or

$$R = F + C + T$$

The formula says that Revenue equals salespeople doing a lot (Frequency) of good things (Competency) in a timely manner (Time). So the theory goes that if you track the items related to frequency, competency, and time, you can ProActively influence revenue. How do you do that? Welcome to the Miller 17.

The Miller 17 was introduced in *ProActive Sales Management* and in Mistake #10 of this book, but this one has a time dimension, so we'll call this the Miller 17 Version 2.0. Like the original Miller 17, version 2.0 is a way for you to ProActively track what salespeople and managers are doing to cause revenue to happen. Figure 17-6 is a good example.

With the time dimension added, you now can predict what activities, competencies, and time elements will determine success for each individual.

In this example, a Miller 17 is used as a management overview divided into four segments (Revenue, Competencies, Frequencies, and Time) over five salespeople. This example is a quarterly representation but could be monthly, depending on the manager's requirements. Under each segment, there is a list of manager's ideas or assessments that the manager believes are necessary for the revenue or results to come in.

Second Quarter Reviews					
1–5 Scale (1 = Low—5 = Excellent)	#1	#2	#3	#4	#5
PERFORMANCE	**2.2**	**3.4**	**2.4**	**3.4**	**3.4**
SALES Y-T-D	2	3	3	4	4
SALES QUARTER REVIEW	2	3	2	4	2
NEW SALES	3	2	1	3	5
RETENTION SALES	2	4	4	3	2
MARGIN SALES	2	5	2	3	4
SALES COMPETENCY	**2.8**	**4.2**	**2.2**	**3.5**	**4.5**
SALES-CYCLE CONTROL	3	4	2	2	5
PRESENTATION SKILLS	3	4	2	4	5
SALES FOCUS	3	5	2	2	4
PRODUCT KNOWLEDGE	2	3	4	5	4
EFFICIENT RESOURCE UTILIZATION	2	5	2	3	4
CUSTOMER KNOWLEDGE	4	4	1	5	5
FREQUENCY	**4.0**	**3.3**	**2.2**	**2.8**	**4.7**
ACCOUNT PENETRATION	2	3	2	4	5
TERRITORY PLAN	4	2	1	2	4
CUSTOMER SUPPORT	3	3	4	3	4
WEEKLY ACTIVITY	5	4	2	3	5
FIELD-TIME MAXIMIZATION	5	4	2	2	5
CALLS PER WEEK	5	4	2	3	5
TIME	**4.3**	**1.7**	**2.7**	**3.0**	**3.0**
TIME-TO-CALL HIGH	5	2	2	3	2
NEW-PRODUCT INTRODUCTIONS	5	1	4	3	2
QUALIFICATION TIME	3	2	2	3	5

Figure 17-6. The Miller 17 Version 2.0.

Salesperson #1 in Figure 17-6 is not doing well, and the performance line shows it. He is getting twos and threes out of a high score of five. Time to break out *the management speech*—you know, the "Sales Motivation 101" talk that you have at the ready for just these occasions. It includes phrases such as, "Sales is a numbers game" and "You have to make customer calls, not internal calls." That type of speech.

If you take a look at the first salesperson's frequencies, you can see he *is* out in the field, getting fives in the Field-Time Maximization and Calls per Week categories. He is calling high and doing so in a timely manner. But take a look at his competencies. Product Knowledge and Efficient Resource Utilization are getting twos. He is a rookie salesperson who is trying very hard but just not knowing what to say.

These Rs, Fs, Cs, and Ts can change over time. It is a good idea to change one or two per period to keep it current and to ensure the manager is predicting what will be needed for success in the coming three to six months.

As Figure 17-6 shows, the manager has done an evaluation of five salespeople. It's a pretty straightforward process, and in this example, the salespeople are ranked on a scale of one to five (five being well above expectations, four being right at expectations, three meaning very close to expectations, two meaning "we have to talk," and a one meaning "we _really_ have to talk").

Let's take a look at some examples to validate the Miller 17 as a ProActive measuring tool.

You now know what to do. You know where to spend your time wisely. Armed with this information, your time is better spent on increasing compe-

Look at the Competencies and Frequencies for Salesperson #2. This is a good salesperson who did not work a plan this quarter and did not want to sell the new product, which justifies the low scores for Territory Plan and Product Knowledge. So because these areas are deficient, guess what the New Sales score is going to look like. You guessed right, it'll be low. This salesperson scored a two in the New Sales category. Validate this with the Time scores, and you get a pretty good idea of what needs to get done. The Miller 17 can predict future and current revenue/performance based on Frequencies, Competencies, and Time elements.

Look at Salesperson #5. Retention Sales and Sales Quarter Review scores are low. But otherwise, this is obviously a good salesperson and the results do point out that revenue is down. Time to go crank her up so she sells more. Time to taunt her with the old, "Well how come no one else is having the same problem?" speech. That will make her more productive, right?

But if you look at her frequencies and competencies, you'll see she is doing the right things and really just had a bad quarter. Look at the Time assessment and you'll see a possible explanation. Was she high enough with that account she lost, or did she stay low where she was comfortable?

If anything, reassure her she is doing the right things from a frequency and competency standpoint. She will break through and bring in the results again. Show her your time scores. Get her agreement on what needs to get done. How do you know? Your Fs, Cs, and Ts are telling you so.

---

tencies than giving "Frequency 101" speeches. The Miller 17 will point to exactly the areas in which you need to focus your time, effort, and energy for this salesperson as well as all the others.

Here are some additional rules for using your Miller 17:

- Take each area on its own merit; the sum score is meaningless. You want the salesperson to concentrate on selected areas, not on an overall ranking.

- Do the R first. It will set an accurate picture in your mind of current performance. Then you can move on to the C, F, and T metrics, which are your rankings of what behaviors you want the salesperson to work on (in the future) rather than focusing on R (the past).

- Use your name to personalize the tool. Call it the Smith 16 or the Jones 18. If your last name is Miller, go ahead and use it.

- Have between 12 and 15 Rs, Fs, Cs, and Ts. Try to avoid having the Smith 44 or the Jones 3. Twelve to 15 variables will focus in on the right number of categories.

- Figure out how you want to introduce this tool to your sales team. You may choose to give the salespeople a blank sheet and have them fill it out to compare to yours. You may want to work on it together. You may also choose to drop it off in their mailboxes and leave town for a few days. You may need the shock value.

- Use the scores to track performance over time—and compliment consistent good performance. Consider this a consistent communication vehicle you are using to inform and gain agreement with your sales team on how it is doing. It is a list of useful, mutually agreed-to, measurable objectives over time. We have a tendency to focus on what's wrong and take for granted—at least in formal communication—our good, consistent performers and what they are doing right.

- Use the scores as documentation for formal corrective action procedures. You are measuring each salesperson to a metric in which all members of the sales team are being held accountable.

- Be consistent and timely in your reviews. Try to make it a habit. Get together the first week of every quarter or the last Monday of every month. People have a normal tendency to fear surprises, especially when they are being evaluated.

- It should take you about 20 to 30 minutes to prepare and complete all the evaluations. Go with your gut feel and adjust if you have to in the one-on-one meetings.

- Let the salesperson participate. You may think he deserves a three in a certain category, but he is adamant about receiving a four ranking. Go ahead and give him a four. People will have a tendency to focus on this issue because they "won." But who really wins if the task gets the right amount of attention?

- Customize it. If you give a two ranking to a C performer, that does not necessarily mean you have to use the same measuring standard for everyone else. The C's two is not necessarily the same standard against which you will be measuring the A player.

- You may want to give an A player a two in an area on which you want her to focus her attention. Compared to the C player, however, she is still a five. Do you give her a five because compared to the C player she is that much better? You can do what you want to on an individual basis, but it will carry more impact if you customize. You are measuring each salesperson on that person's own unique abilities and performance, not making a comparison with anyone else on the team. The Miller 17 is the true measure of the skills and levels at which each person performs, not a comparison of salespeople to one another.

- A players will love this tool, C players will hate it. There's no place to hide.

- If you are a second- or third-level manager, make sure you do a Miller 17 on your managers. They want feedback too.

Managers need to have a way to measure the future. They need to communicate formally, both to their salespeople and their bosses, the competencies, frequencies, and time elements of the sales team.

The communication of measurements to salespeople is invaluable. It lets them know what behavior is expected of them in the future. It tells them how to succeed.

For managers, it is a mutual communications vehicle that allows them to do the specific tasks required to get the job done. To senior managers, it describes the state of the sales team—its current deficiencies and overall trends. It will pinpoint low-scoring areas that may need management attention or added resources. Here's the bottom line: It is very effective to have a manager ProActively manage a sales team on one piece of paper.

Forecasting to
60 Percent Accuracy

"The forecast is not looking too bad."

It's a simple phrase, but it haunts managers. You can see the fear in their eyes. Here is a better motto to live by:

> **Yes's are great; no's are great too.**
> **It's the maybe's that will kill you.**

When it comes to forecasting, no one really does it right, whatever right is. But forecasting revenue is obviously a prime responsibility of the sales-management team. Management makes many mistakes in this area. The top three are:

1. Believing the salesperson
2. A lack of a forecasting process
3. Single-dimension forecasting

BELIEVING THE SALESPERSON

Your salesperson says some deal is going to come in within the next three weeks. You want to believe him; he wants to believe the customer. Everyone wants to believe everyone. One happy organization.

So the question is, what do you believe? It's generally good to assume that salespeople are speaking the truth as they believe it, but not when it comes down to a predictable Buy/Sales process. Oh, yeah, that thing you are supposed to measure sales against.

Belief in the sales team is good. It inspires them and makes the management team look good. However (and this is a big however), it is not the right thing to do when forecasting.

A LACK OF A FORECASTING PROCESS

Selling without a process is like sailing a ship without a rudder. The Buy/Sell forecasting process will allow you and your sales team to measure itself and put the responsibility for the process where it belongs—at the salesperson level. That way, the management team can work the process, not be worked over by it.

The elements of a good forecasting model are:

- Account Name and Division—Who is making the purchase.

- Salesperson—The salesperson or sales team on this account, as well as the regional manager.

- Sales Process Stage—Where a deal is in the sales process.

- History Tracking—Not only how long is a deal in the funnel, but how long has it been in each stage; this is a reflection of deal management and stage velocity.

- Deal Size—How much the customer plans on spending with you.

- Close Date/I-Date—When the customer is going to take delivery of what you are selling or when the customer will use it and when you can take credit for it.

- Products/Services Being Sold—This is self-explanatory.

Take this information and use it to forecast your business without a lot of risks in the business model for fear of the business slipping, being lost, or just plain disappearing from sight.

A sample of a good forecast is shown in Figure 18-1. This is a revised version of the 30-60-90 report from *ProActive Sales Management*. If you need a basic forecasting tool, this might be for you.

Figure 18-1 is a basic sales forecast, but it also tracks the sales stage. Only accounts that are above Stage 5, and really Stage 6, can go above the line for the forecast.

Here are some other rules for the 30-60-90 forecasting tool:

- *The report must be mutually beneficial.* A report that does not have value to the sales manager as well as the salesperson will suffer in its accuracy, no matter how hard you insist on it. The report should be focused on what it is intended to do.

- *Gather input weekly.* Get your details on a timely basis.

- *Keep it simple.* "Well, if we could add just one or two more things to the report . . ." has killed many good reports.

- *Use the 80/20 rule.* This is a forecast report, and the value of the report is in its timeliness. Use the 80/20 rule for this report. The salespeople should not have to forecast to the exact dollar amount as long as they are close. Limit the forecast to anything under a certain dollar amount that you believe to be insignificant, say under $10,000 or $15,000. This is another insurance policy for the sales manager.

- *Make the input easy for the salespeople to use.* It should take them no more than 15 minutes per week to fill out a 30-60-90 report.

- *The input must be controlled by a neutral third party, such as an administrator or the manager.* Allowing the salespeople to update a master report on a monthly basis permits them to cut a few "maybe's" that are beginning to look bad. The whole idea is to track the maybe's, not sweep them under the rug!

- *Reports must be submitted on a timely basis.* Everyone should adhere to a deadline, say noon on Friday. Those who miss the deadline should be disciplined in a consistent, timely, and fair manner.

- *Once a line item on the report is completed (either won or lost), the line item should be removed and a new one, if*

Salesperson - Debbie Jones
Week End - January 3

ProActive Selling Sales Phase
1- Initial Interest
2- Educate
3- MMM
4- Demonstration
5- Validate
6- Propose
7- Close

Bold - Business won
X - Business lost
$0 - Forecast slip
Duration - Weeks in Sales Cycle

FY 2000

Forecast

Account	Product	Stage	Duration	Jan	Feb	Mar	Apr	May	Jun	Jul	Aug	Sep	Comments
Account	Gas	6	1		$17,000								
Account	Gas	6	2	$55,900									
Account	Light 1	6	2		$23,400								
Account	Light 1	6	1			$17,500							
Account	Light 1	5	2			$33,000							
Account	Inspector	7	2		$12,400								
Account	Gadget	7	1		$12,900								
Account	Gas	7	1		$20,000								
Account	Suite	6	2			$15,000							
Account	Suite	6	1			$63,000							
Totals by Month				$55,900	$85,700	$128,500	$0	$0	$0	$0	$0	$0	
Totals by Quarter						$270,100			$0			$0	
Quota						$200,000			$200,000			$200,000	
% of Quota by Quarter						135.05%			0.00%			0.00%	

Funnel

Account	Product	Stage	Duration	Jan	Feb	Mar	Apr	May	Jun	Jul	Aug	Sep	Comments
Account	Stopwatch	6	2		$16,700								
Account	Stopwatch	5	1				$63,000						
Account	Inspector	5	4		$0	$66,000							
Account	Gas	3	2					$44,800					
Account	Gas	4	3				$22,000						
Account	Gas	5	1					$15,000					
Account	Gadget	5	2			$0	$21,900						
Account	Stopwatch	4	3			$11,000							
Projected Totals				$0	$16,700	$77,000	$106,900	$59,800	$0	$0	$0	$0	

Prospects

Account	Date Start	Status	Comments
Account	1-Jan	1	
Account	1-Jan	1	
Account	2-Jan	1	
Account	2-Feb	2	
Account	14-Feb	2	
Account	28-Mar	1	

Figure 18-1. A sample forecast.

applicable, inserted in its place. This report should not be used for total sales year-to-date (YTD), sales by product YTD, or anything YTD. It is a rolling "balance sheet" report. Sales management has a host of other reports that detail YTD items, such as sales by customer YTD, sales by product YTD, won/loss reports, and so on. (A quick word on won/loss reports: Do not expect salespeople to be 100 percent truthful. Most of the time, when they lose a deal, it's because they got outsold. But the comment column on the report will show only their rationalization of why they lost. Besides, why are you taking so much time tracking losses when you should be tracking wins so you can repeat successful behavior?)

The 30-60-90 report is broken up into three zones: Forecast, Funnel, and Prospects. Only the Forecast zone is allowed to be used for forecasting against quotas. Funnel and Prospects are for the manager to view the sales pipeline only. The key is for the salesperson to update the report weekly and do one of three things to the report:

1. *Identify business won.* In Figure 18-1, the salesperson has bolded the account's dollar amount.

2. *Identify business lost.* These are identified by an "x" in the report.

3. *Identify maybe's.* A "$0" has been placed in the column for these accounts, the ones that keep slipping every month.

At the end of the month, the salesperson must choose what action needs to be taken with the accounts on the report—won, lost, or slip (maybe). The salesperson must choose, not the manager. Forecast accuracy is the salesperson's responsibility, not the manager's.

In the report, you can also track where in the sales cycle the salesperson is with a certain account. The report in Figure 18-2 uses the sales-cycle terminology of ProActive Selling™, an M3 Learning sales program that lets the salesperson control the sales cycle and master qualification skills to eliminate maybe's. This enables focused communication between the salesperson and the sales manager. You can use this or one of your own. The goal is to identify a process and measure to it.

The previous 30-60-90 was an example of a good report. Let's look at a report (Figure 18-2) done by a salesperson who is not doing well.

Salesperson - Debbie Jones
Week End - April 30

ProActive Selling Sales Phase

1 - Initial Interest	5 - Validate
2 - Educate	6 - Propose
3 - MMM	7 - Close
4 - Demonstration	

Bold - Business won	
X - Business lost	
$0 - Forecast slip	

FY 2007

Forecast

Account	Product	Stage	Duration	Jan	Feb	Mar	Apr	May	Jun	Comments
Account	Light 7	7	1	$55,900	$17,000			$34,000		
Account	Light 3	7	3					$26,900		
Account	Light 5	6	2		x		$23,000			
Account	Light 15	5	2			$17,500			$77,000	
Account	Light 1	5	5		$12,400	$33,000			$54,000	
TCFS	YYY	7	4		$0	$0 x	$0	$30,000		
Account	Gas	7	4		$0	$0	$0	$20,000		
Account	Suite	6	6			$15,000		$63,000		
Account						$0	$23,000 x			
Totals by Month				$55,900	$29,400	$65,500	$23,000	$110,900	$131,000	
Totals by Quarter						$150,800			$264,900	
Quota						$200,000			$200,000	
% of Quota by Quarter						75.40%			132.45%	

Funnel

Account	Product	Stage	Duration	Jan	Feb	Mar	Apr	May	Jun	Comments
Account	Stopwatch	6	2						$12,000	
Account	Stopwatch	5	4				$63,000			
Account	Inspector	5	2						$33,000	
Account	Gas	3	3					$44,800		
Account	Gas	5	3				$22,000			
Account	Gas	4	2					$15,000		
Account	Gadget	6	1				$21,900			
Account	Stopwatch	4	4			$0				
Projected Totals				$0	$0	$11,000	$106,900	$59,800	$45,000	

Prospects

Account	Product	Date Start	Status							Comments
Account		1-Jan	1							
Account		1-Jan	1							
Account		2-Jan	1							

Figure 18-2. A sample report for an underperforming salesperson.

As you can see, the report is telling.

- The large number of X marks indicates the salesperson has forecasted revenue in these months. At the end of each month, the salesperson had to make a decision to either close, slip, or lose the forecasted deal. It could not just "vanish" from the list.

- The large number of slips indicates a low probability of close potential. This salesperson needs help in forecasting and probably in qualifying a potential deal. The sales manager should use the Miller 17 to highlight key areas of Frequency, Competency, and Time elements. Coaching can begin on a ProActive basis instead of waiting a few months for a quarterly review.

- After three or four months, the $0 slips decrease in their probability of closing. A general rule of thumb is that if an account is on the 30-60-90 report Forecast for more than two months, it should be given an X and taken off the report or dropped down to Funnel or Prospect. With a 6 or 7 in the sales stage, you should be wondering whether this salesperson needs to go back and start the deal over again.

The 30-60-90 weekly report allows the sales manager to take aggressive action on a monthly basis and reward on a quarterly basis accordingly. For some companies, it may be beneficial to do the report on a daily/weekly/monthly basis. For other situations, a monthly/quarterly/semiannual basis is acceptable. Some companies use units as a measure instead of dollars. Use any measurable unit or timeframe you feel you need to be successful, *but track the maybe's.*

A sound 30-60-90 report:

- Gives both parties timely input into the sales-forecast method

- Tracks performance by salesperson

- Holds the appropriate parties (salespeople) accountable

- Identifies failings (Xs and $0s) ProActively

- Provides a useful coaching tool when combined with the Miller 17

- Tracks the *maybe's*

Remember, you are not tracking history. You are forecasting the future. As such, you can forget about updating past months for exact dollar accuracy. This tool is for keeping a future-based, rolling 30-60-90-day forecast in line with expectations. Stay focused on the current month and the next two months. Figure 18-3 provides an example.

ABC Co.	Week 3	Week 4
Stage 3	$7,145	$6,300
Stage 4	$3,540	$2,800
Stage 5	$3,115	$1,125
Stage 6	$4,550	$5,335
Total	$18,350	$15,560

Figure 18-3. Forecasting financial performance.

A final note for sales organizations that use distributors and independent sales reps (i.e., salespeople who do not work directly for the company): The 30-60-90 tool is a welcome addition because it keeps the business relationship in line with business expectations. You have a right to know, based on the time and money your are spending, how your investment is paying off and how both parties can help keep the relationship profitable.

● FORECASTING THE MAYBES ●

So with the 30-60-90, you have a great deal of information that is mutually beneficial. The key to a great sales-forecasting process is to track and control the largest variable. That would be the *maybe's*. The 30-60-90 was designed to track the maybe's.

Forecasting also has to do with velocity, or the speed of travel through the Buy/Sales process. Why? What does this tell you about a sale's probability?

Let's go back to the original funnel-management discussion. What is a good sales funnel? Again, when you are looking at size and shape, you have two variables and can do some keen observation. Look at the sales funnels in Figure 18-4. This company has a seven-step sales cycle and can track its activity visually. These are the results from two equal sales regions. Given the two funnels, what can you conclude? What do these funnels mean?

A.   Your price may be too high because things are sitting in the funnel.

B.   You may want to compare this funnel with some norms.

C.   You better get more in the funnel.

D.   Stage 5 is where the trouble is.

E.   All of the above.

F.   None of the above.

Look at it again before you read forward and see the answer. Look at the differences among stages.

Okay, the answer is F, none of the above. You as a sales manager are so interested in data and what the shape and the size of the funnel is that you are missing a key ingredient: speed.

Funnel #1   **Funnel #2**

Figure 18-4. Funnel management.

Here are your choices again. Same funnel, different quiz.

A. Funnel #1 has too much stuff in Level 4. The salespeople are not doing a good job of qualifying potential customers.

B. Funnel #2 is very slim, so the process works. The salespeople may need to fatten up the early stages to get more prospects in the funnel.

C. Funnel #1 is in trouble. How can they manage so many prospects in the early part of the funnel?

D. Funnel #2 is in trouble. They are not hunting actively.

E. All of the above.

F. None of the above.

No suspense this time. The answer again is F, none of the above. Why? What data is missing to make some sound management decisions?

Yes, you can tell a few things about the funnels side by side, so some of the earlier answers hold water. But without understanding velocity, or the speed of the levels, what good are the funnels?

Take a look at the funnels in Figure 18-5. What can you conclude?

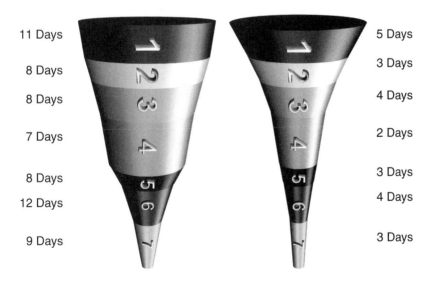

11 Days		5 Days
8 Days		3 Days
8 Days		4 Days
7 Days		2 Days
8 Days		3 Days
12 Days		4 Days
9 Days		3 Days

Funnel #1—Team A   Funnel #2—Team B

Figure 18-5. The funnels for team A and team B.

So team A takes 63 days to close an average sale, but team B takes 24 days. If the average sales price (ASP) for a deal is $20,000, and team B is closing three times the number of deals that team A is closing, then team B is going to finish ahead of the game by a wide margin.

Now, if team B does not keep the funnel loaded on top, it is going to have some issues. Team A better qualify faster, as well as shorten the time in between levels.

Assume that both teams were able to go through the funnel in 24 days, as shown in Figure 18-6. What conclusions would you draw?

Now the picture looks very different. Look at all the touches team A is having with the customer. It is doing a great job hitting as many customers as it can. It makes you wonder about team B, doesn't it? Sure, it is doing a great job, but is it really getting market share? Is it taking only the "low-hanging fruit"?

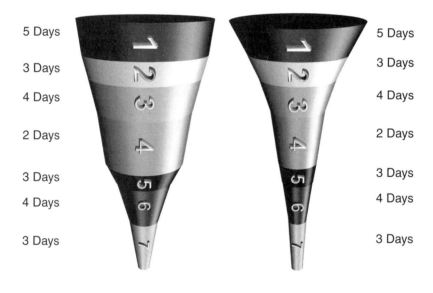

5 Days		5 Days
3 Days		3 Days
4 Days		4 Days
2 Days		2 Days
3 Days		3 Days
4 Days		4 Days
3 Days		3 Days

Funnel #1—Team A   **Funnel #2—Team B**

Figure 18-6. Funnel management #2.

> ### The CFO
>
> *"I thought he was my friend," said the sales VP. "I thought he would be happy that we are going to measure the sales team in a faster way so we can reward the good salespeople faster and get rid of the poor performers faster."*
>
> *"'My systems are not ready for it, and I do not see the benefits,' the CFO told me. Sounds like he had other problems he was dealing with, and my sales productivity improvements were not on the top of his list.*
>
> *"Four months later, and with some major convincing at the CFO level, we have monthly sales quotas, compensation, and quarterly territory readjustments in place. The compensation was easy; they were getting paid monthly. Sales quotas were not that hard either.*
>
> *"Now we're making the quarterly territory reassignments and selling this whole idea to the sales team; this is interesting.*
>
> *"We finally drew a line in the sand. Each salesperson could carry 30 accounts. At the end of the quarter, each was allowed to pick 30 accounts in her territory, then the rest had to go into a house account, where the new hires or the members of the inside sales team were now in charge of these accounts.*
>
> *"No more accounts where a salesperson has been on it for four years and got nothing new. It pays to keep the most active ones, not the biggest, and for our business, this was key.*
>
> *"The CFO . . . he likes me. We have made the number the last seven quarters, and I make sure he gets the credit."*

THE FINAL LOOK

Figure 18-7 is a 30-60-90 report that includes velocity issues. Dark gray marks business lost, light gray marks slips. You do the math. Based on days in sales and days in stage, is Debbie going to make the second quarter? Look at the funnel. Debbie has some coaching in her future.

There may not be a huge advantage for senior managers to use the 30-60-90 sheets every week, but in monthly or quarterly reviews, they are probably invaluable. The funnel and funnel management of velocity is probably a huge issue for you if you are seeking answers to the following questions:

- Why are my sales taking so long?
- Why are the deals getting stuck?

Salesperson - Debbie Jones
Week End - April 30
ProActive Selling Sales Phase
1- Initial Interest
2- Educate
3- MMM
4- Demonstration
5- Validate
6- Propose
7- Close

Bold - Business won
X - Business lost
$0 - Forecast slip

					FY 2007						
Account	**Product**	**Stage**	**Duration/Stage**	**Duration in Sale**	**Jan**	**Feb**	**Mar**	**Apr**	**May**	**Jun**	**Comments**
Forecast											
Account	Light 7	7	1	6		$17,000			$34,000		
Account	Light 3	7	3	5	$55,900	x			$26,900		
Account	Light 5	6	2	5				$23,000			
Account	Light 15	5	2	6			$17,500			$77,000	
Account	Light 1	5	5	5			$33,000			$54,000	
TCFS	YYY	7	4	12		$12,400	$0 x	$0	$30,000		
Account	Gas	7	4	14		$0	$0	$20,000			
Account	Suite	6	6	14			$15,000	$0	$63,000		
							$23,000 x	$23,000 x			
Totals by Month					$55,900	$29,400	$65,500	$23,000	$110,900	$131,000	
Totals by Quarter							$150,800			$264,900	
Quota							$200,000			$200,000	
% of Quota by Quarter							75.40%			132.45%	

Account	**Product**	**Stage**	**Duration/Stage**		**Jan**	**Feb**	**Mar**	**Apr**	**May**	**Jun**	**Comments**
Funnel											
Account	Stopwatch	6	2							$12,000	
Account	Stopwatch	5	4					$63,000			
Account	Inspector	5	2							$33,000	
Account	Gas	3	3						$44,800		
Account	Gas	5	3					$22,000	$15,000		
Account	Gadget	6	1				$0	$21,900			
Account	Stopwatch	4	4				$11,000				
Projected Totals					$0	$0	$11,000	$106,900	$59,800	$45,000	

Account	**Date Start**	**Status**									**Comments**
Prospects											
Acount	1-Jan	1									
Account	1-Jan	1									
Account	2-Jan	1									

Figure 18-7. A 30-60-90 sheet with velocity issues.

- Are we leaving money on the table?

- Are we going broad and deep early enough?

- If we do close an account early, how long does it take to get the second, larger sale? Should we have gone after the whole sale, or is it better in pieces?

If these are questions that are nagging at the back of your mind—or even at the front of it—you have to get in front of the speed issue. *Maybe's* will kill you, and the speed at which you control your funnel, not just the funnel itself, will give you great insight into what is going on at the sales level—and what you can do about it.

FOURTH-QUARTER PLANNING

Much has been said about the demise of annual quotas. Time and time again, the managers I speak with are very hesitant to break away from an annual metric and pay system. Time and time again, however, we hear that once managers make the jump to a quarterly or monthly pay and quota system, they wonder what took them so long. Do it now.

MISTAKE

The Stack Ranking Behind Hire and Fire Decisions

> "I can hire two types of people: people who are smarter than I am, or people who are stupider. I prefer the first but seem to get the second. Why?"
>
> "It seems to take my regional managers one week to hire a C player and about nine months to get rid of them. How can we do this whole hire-fire thing better?"
>
> "My better is better than your better."
> —NIKE AD

<u>What does it take to pull together a better sales team than the one you have now?</u> That's the million-dollar question. How do you make the team better and keep the culture going in the right direction? If you are a first-line sales manager, has anyone told you how to hire and execute corrective action effectively, or are you learning on the job?

If you are a second- or third-line manager, you do not have the time to sit in on interviews of all new hires. Who has taught you how to develop a process for adding to and subtracting from the sales ranks in a ProActive manner.

Anyone can hire a competitor's A player and fire the salesperson who has not been performing, especially if that person has not been performing for three years. The trick is, how do you implement a system or a process that can do it better?

Well first, it takes a game plan.

THE GAME PLAN

There is a certain hockey team in the town where I live. The team has done very well for years. Always in the top of the league, they usually win quite a few playoff games. They have not won it all, but they have come close. By most measures, the team has done well as an organization, certainly from a bottom-line-profit measure.

I once read a fascinating news article about this team. The interviewer asked the team's general manager how he consistently kept them in contention. He asked about adding key people late in the season and how they fit in so well with the team.

Specifically, he wanted to understand how, toward the end of the season and before the final trade deadline, the GM knew whether a new player would fit into the team culture and be a net addition to the organization.

"Well," said the GM, "In my office I have a whiteboard shaped like a hockey arena, and on it is listed the players, their positions, and what they bring to the table as far as their strengths and weaknesses. I then have next to the positions what areas are needed for this team to succeed. So now when a player who can come closer to what we need becomes available, we go after them. It's really not magic; it's just comparing what is available to what we need. We spend a lot of time detailing what we need. We have a game plan. That's the difference."

Where is your game plan? You can be ProActive and assess your current team. There are many assessment firms that will come in and interview the management of the organization to help determine what skill sets the sales managers and salespeople need. They can assess the skills of the individuals in each position; then you'll have a baseline. No, you are not going to trade for a better player, but you are in a position to create ProActive training opportunities and give promotions. If you know what you need, you can help the employees get there. So where is your game plan?

Make sure you spend some time projecting what you need at each position over the next six months so you have accurate guides. Figure 19-1 is an example of a game plan a second-line manager might create.

Sales Team Game Plan

Sales Team:_____   For the Year: _____

The overall assessment of the sales team over the next 6 months is:

Double-digit growth	Increased executive contact and executive sales approach
Geographic expansion	Partnering opportunities
Solutions orientation in the sales approach	Increased ASP by 40 percent

We have _____ sales managers. The skills great sales managers have are:

Great interviewing and hiring skills	Ability to work with other managers
Coaching for executive selling	Provide leadership to marketing dept.
Solutions approach for major opportunities	Provide leadership to A players

We have _____ national salespeople. The skills these salespeople have are:

Ability to go broad and deep in an account	Ability to work in a sales process
Executive-selling skills	Business skill set
Ability to work with partners and increase opportunity	Provide leadership to team

We have _____ inside salespeople. The skills these salespeople have are:

Lead-generation skills at all levels	Uncover customers' real needs
Positive work ethic	Time-management/organization skills
Ability to dig out opportunities quickly	Master qualification process

Figure 19-1. An example of a game plan.

Creating the game plan is harder than you think. It should represent what you believe are the requirements necessary for success at each position in the organization. Figure 19-1 addresses a national outside sales team and an inside sales team, but you should come up with your own list that represents your sales organization.

After you put that together, then assess your organization. Again, you can use a professional assessment firm, or you can create a list of employees and rank how they perform to the needed skill sets you require.

Figure 19-2 is a sample assessment of John Smith, who is a great salesperson, but in the areas of executive selling and working a sales process, he could use some coaching, outside training, mentoring, or guidance. He's a great fit now and in the future.

Ability to go broad and deep in an account—A	Ability to work in a sales process—B–
Executive-selling skills—B	Business skill set—A
Ability to work with partners and increase opportunity—A	Provide leadership to team—A

Figure 19-2. John Smith—National Salesperson—2009 Assessment.

Gerry makes his number every year. He's not an outstanding salesperson, but he makes his number. He does not want to get "any training on new things" and really is a lone wolf type of salesperson. His assessment is in Figure 19.3.

Ability to go broad and deep in an account—A	Ability to work in a sales process—C
Executive-selling skills—C	Business skill set—B–
Ability to work with partners and increase opportunity—C	Provide leadership to team—C

Figure 19-3. Gerry Gold—National Salesperson—2009 Assessment.

In most organizations, Gerry would be left alone and the management team would be looking elsewhere for additions and improvements. This assessment tells you otherwise. It is up to you to take some action. Gerry is not getting all he can out of the territory. Sales management needs to:

- Insist on some training
- Cut the territory Gerry is responsible for

- Give Gerry something else to do

- Show Gerry what is not being covered and work with him on new goals

- Work Gerry out of the organization

The productivity gap that most sales organizations have is enormous because most sales organizations do not have a metric for what skills are needed for success. They hire piecemeal, but they expect team results.

Yes, each sales territory and each management position is unique, and that's why you create the Profile of a Successful Performer. However, not having a game plan for the overall direction of your sales team means you have an unleveraged part of your organization.

We have heard from a few managers who actually have a hiring game plan. Most of them are in high-growth areas; they will double their sales teams inside of three years. They claim that without a game plan, their sales teams had a 24 percent churn annually. With a game plan, they are now below 12 percent. Hey, if a sales game plan can work with them, why wouldn't it work for you?

INTERVIEWING MISTAKES

The number of interviewing and hiring mistakes sales managers have made over the years is not very long. It seems that when it comes to hiring, managers just keep making the same mistakes over and over again. For interviewing, the list breaks down into two distinct categories:

1. Not enough candidates in the funnel

2. Bad interviewing skills

Not Enough Candidates in the Funnel

Much has been written about the time needed to find good sales candidates. After all, you are only as good as the pool of available resources. Some managers are known to block off one day a month—a whole day, not just a morning—for finding and recruiting candidates. This is in addition to having recruiters, placing ads, doing Web searches, and the like. Look at your calendar and block off the time. Now the question is: What will you do with that time?

- Network

- Tell some friends you are looking

- Go to a local trade show and see some people working booths

- Talk to some recruiters

- Search the Web

Managers I have spoken with claim the number-one problem with hiring is the lack of good talent. But when asked, they say they are doing little or nothing outside of hiring a recruiter to get them talent. Go figure. Do you even know any websites that salespeople frequent? Go ask your salespeople—your good ones. They'll tell you.

The number-one rule for managers is that there is nothing worse than an open head count. Nothing. If you are a first-line manager, having open territory without a salesperson in it is getting you further and further behind the number.

If you are a second-line sales manager, having empty manager positions minimizes the importance of the position, and so on up the line. It is not hard to find good people. Good people are always looking for good opportunities. You just have to work at it. I know of a company that had an open first-line manager position for 22 months. Now there's a message in there somewhere.

You will be amazed at what you can accomplish when you put your mind to it. Hey, didn't your Mom used to say that?

So a manager who was looking for two salespeople relates a bet he made with his boss. The manager was explaining the lack of good talent to the boss. The boss claimed there was quite a bit of talent out there and that the manager was not being ProActive in his search. The boss bet the manager he could get a pool of five great candidates in a week.

The boss went to the Web and searched local trade events and local trade shows relevant to his industry; he found there were two in his area that week. He took a stack of business cards and went to the shows. He spent three hours passing out business cards at one show, and he spent two hours at the other. By Friday, he had received 17 e-mails from people to whom he had passed out business cards.

He phoned all 17 and brought 9 in for an interview on Friday. By Friday night he had generated a list of 4 candidates he thought were highly qualified. He wasn't about to make the hiring decision—that was the manager's job. So, the manager won the bet, but the boss won his point.

Bad Interviewing Skills

I have heard from way too many managers on this one, and I have classified these hiring mistakes into seven categories.

Mistake #1: Hiring Based Only on Skills, Ability, and Experience. You are really interested in the candidate's behavior and work ethic, which you believe you will glean from the interview. Without proper preparation—knowing exactly what you want the candidate to do and how she will approach issues—why are you interviewing the person?

Too often managers are impressed with an individual's background and accomplishments. The interviewer builds rapport with the prospect, and based on that believes the interview went well. Once the hiring manager decides he likes the candidate, the interviewer will look for things to validate this feeling rather than take an objective look. In general, the candidate's references and feedback from others in the organization who interview the candidate will help validate the manager's initial feelings.

Sometimes the hiring manager actually acts surprised when someone comes back with mixed reviews, and then the manager discounts that interviewer. "What do they know about sales anyway?" is the comment heard most often.

Look at an interview as a video, not a snapshot. How will this candidate look over the long term with all the daily tasks that are required? Don't just consider the nice smile or warm personality.

Mistake #2: Using the Interview as the Major Hiring Tool. Did you know that using an interview as the sole hiring criteria increases the odds of making a good hire by only 2 percent? That's it. There is so much subjective thinking in an interview—"How do I like this candidate?"—that the real impact of a typical interview increases your chances of hiring well by just 2 percent. Here are some of the most common reasons managers think subjectively instead of objectively.

1. They have no prepared interview checklist.

2. They are looking at what the candidate wants them to see, rather than looking for fit.

3. Their interviews confirm rapport and "likeability." They really do nothing to help learn about the candidate's ability to do the job.

It turns out the best thing a hiring manager can do to increase the odds of success is to complete a Profile Sheet, as shown in Figure 19-4. A Profile Sheet makes you think about the interview as if it were a video. It forces hiring managers to ask themselves questions such as, "What are the characteristics I am looking for in this candidate based on what he needs to be doing?" This is the only way you will be able to compare candidates on standards against which you are measuring success.

Profile of a Successful Performer

Job:
Name

Job Skills and Knowledge	Desirable Qualities
Communication skills	Early riser
Industry knowledge—some	Leadership
Territory management	Relates well to others
Negotiation skills of $100K and above	Careful with detail
International knowledge	Sees "big picture"

Magic Seven

Natural Curiosity
Complex to Simple
Quiet Competence
Ability to Flip
All 3 Perspectives
Works a Process
Loves a Challenge

Background: Experience and Education	Will Enjoy Doing
5+ years in sales	Prospecting
Calling high	Calling high
Solution sales expertise	Working a sales process
Knows the territory	Traveling
	Using a CRM tool
	Being decisive

Figure 19-4. A sample Profile Sheet.

Okay, Okay, Okay

She took over a new sales team and had her work cut out for her. Fifteen salespeople and three managers, and it seemed at least half the salespeople and at least one of the managers would not make it.

She personally got involved in the first new salesperson hire and made sure they hired the right person.

Two months later, she was having doubts.

"I am not sure on this one. He seemed so great in the interview, but now it just seems he was all talk. The other day, he showed me who he had prospected to. Just for fun, I called three of the numbers, and two were no longer in service. I am having my doubts."

When asked to see her Profile Sheet (she has known about Profile Sheets for a long time), her face turned red.

"Never again will I go into an interview without one. I have learned my lesson. But he seemed like a great hire. Okay, okay, point made."

Sure hope so.

Mistake #3: Trying to Duplicate Success. The world is replete with new employees who were hired because they acted like their bosses and the bosses liked what they saw—this is also called *cloning*. This is *really* prevalent in promotions. The responses I got (some pretty funny) from managers who promoted the wrong candidates were staggering.

- "The sales management mistake I'll never make again is hiring an individual into a sales position because it happens to be that person's 'turn.' And here's why: Obviously the same skills necessary to be efficient in one area may not apply to outside sales. However, you may find yourself rationalizing in situations where candidates are limited in number and feel they are the right person for the job."

- "The sales management mistake I'll never make again is assuming that a great rep with incredible experience will fit into the team."

- "Hiring a sales exec to replace me too quickly after I was promoted. I'm not sure why really; I'm 0 for 2 here."

- "When looking for the best sales candidates, it is easy to become enamored by their skills, knowledge, and experience. When we find one who looks great, we tend to overlook the most important characteristics—behavioral traits. We fail to see because we can overfocus around 'who might help me hit my number now.' We justify based on reasoning such as 'he will hit the ground running' or 'she has a great book of business' or 'he has the domain expertise I have to have in this assignment' and other assorted reasons that make sense in the short term. But, what is the person's work ethic really like? How does the person align with people? How does the person react when things don't go the right way? How does the person deal with customer problems? Is he high or low maintenance? What would past bosses, peers, and subordinates say about her attitude? What would they say about how his past bosses, peers, and subordinates would rate his attitude? Basic information on understanding behavioral traits is paramount.

- "You can teach knowledge and coach skills, but most behavioral traits seem to be 'DNA based.' Without a Ph.D. in genetics, superb surgical skills to restructure the human genome, or a lifetime of psychoanalysis, behavioral traits are pretty hard to change. There is nothing worse than hiring that bright, knowledgeable, and highly skilled individual who ends up being an 'axe murderer' leaving a trail of body parts behind him."

Managers also said they regretted hiring people who acted like junior salespeople. The hiring managers thought they could teach these people, who never really grow up. Some managers hired "repeat performers"—salespeople who were so successful somewhere else that the hiring managers were sure these candidates could have the same success in the manager's organization, since they have done it before and therefore could do it again.

Mistake #4: Too Much to Evaluate—The Law of Seven. It seems like every time you ask people what they are looking for in a sales or sales-management candidate, they can tell you in five or six bullet points. When you look at their homework—the stuff a manager brings into an interview—it is either corporate drivel or it is what they *say* they really want. Either way, it won't help them hire great candidates. Research has proved two things:

- The top two critical factors for predicting success in any job are as important or more important than all other factors combined.

- No more than six to eight criteria are necessary to predict professional success. Seven seems to be the right number. Add any more and you water down your criteria and the ability to predict success.

Come up with the Magic Seven criteria—no more—that will make this hire a success. Then evaluate every candidate with these seven, along with the other items you deem necessary, on the Profile Sheet. Please remember, the Magic Seven listed on the sample Profile Sheet in Figure 19-4 are made up. Take a minute and come up with the seven most important criteria for a candidate to be successful in the job you are offering. Then use them.

Mistake #5: Bad Job Description. This one is easy. Eighty-one percent of hiring managers have no current job descriptions in front of them when they hire. That's a big number. But does it mean that 81 percent of hiring managers have no clue what they are looking for? No. But they'll know their mistake when it sneaks up and bites them again.

Mistake #6: Not Knowing Why People Have Failed. This is very inherent knowledge, and managers tend to blame failure on the candidate or the organization's lack of a good hiring process. Great organizations have also spent time determining what, exactly, made a "great" candidate fail. Then they probe for this behavior in future interviews.

The top three things that cause a "great" candidate to fail are:

- The candidate's inability to multitask

- The candidate's failure to back up his claims

- The hiring manager's lack of clear goals—also called the "They'll figure it out" syndrome

Mistake #7: Not Doing the Reference Check. Up to 20 percent of candidates wash out during the final reference checks, and most of these bad references were given to the prospective employer by the candidates themselves.

Customer and character references are critical in the new-hire process, and I recommend you get at least three, especially customer references. Even at the manager level, this will offer great insight in the evaluation.

MISTAKES DURING THE FIRST 90 DAYS

Managers told me that the biggest mistakes they made during the first 90 days of a new salesperson's employment were:

- They did not give the candidate specific objectives to meet on a weekly basis.
- They did not cut losses after the first 30 days.
- They did not put measurable objectives, other than revenue, in place for a year, which was 11 months too late.

The best thing you can do is have your organization put together the first 90 days of a new-hire process. It should include things candidates can accomplish, people they should meet, and the goals they plan to accomplish within the next 90 days. This may seem very cut and dried, but again, most new hires are "thrown out of the nest" and made to see if they can fly. You can do better.

CORRECTIVE-ACTION MISTAKES

It's the same thing over and over again. It's almost like you know there is trouble, everyone tells you about it, you read about it, and you have even been there before. You know the problem fully, but you stick your hand on the stove for the third time. It can't be hot again. Go figure. Here are the big two mistakes for corrective action:

1. I did not correct the behavior I wanted to correct in a timely manner.

2. I did not fail fast.

The phrase is: If you are going to fail, fail fast. It needs to be heeded. Here are a couple of stories managers told me about learning this lesson.

I won't discipline my sales managers by reprimanding them on an issue. Instead I have learned to use it as a learning experience. I identify the issue and talk through it with them. I make certain we document the situation and schedule follow-up coaching meetings regarding the problem to ensure the same instance doesn't occur again. It gives me an opportunity to coach them in the areas where I know they need help. This is good; I just have to stop waiting three months before I start something.

Not trusting your gut and waiting too long to make a "fire" decision is a mistake. When it looks like a duck, quacks like a duck, and flies like a duck . . . well, it's a duck. You don't need the game warden to tell you so.

SUMMARY

Interviewing, hiring, and corrective action are integral parts of the sales manager's job. As you have seen, when the subjective sneaks into the interview and the hiring process, it can be deadly. When the lack of speed affects corrective action, the effects are just the same. Learn from others' mistakes and you'll be way ahead of the game.

PART FIVE

SELF DECISIONS

> "Creativity is allowing yourself to make mistakes.
> Art is knowing which ones to keep."
> —SCOTT ADAMS, *THE DILBERT PRINCIPLE*

Okay, it is now time to give yourself and your decisions a bit of attention. Culture, time management, authority, and responsibility are on the agenda. You tend to be so locked into meetings and topics that affect employees, peers, or the company, that there really isn't any time for you.

Just like a car: If you don't take it in for maintenance or get a new one every few years, it will break down—and at the worst possible time.

There are still sales organizations out there with no sales process, organizations that still believe—even in this Internet age—that their salespeople do not have time to prospect. There is a lot of work to do. That said, take a breath.

Yes, it's time for a breather. Read a good book. Put some new ideas into your head that actually work.

Time for that tune-up so you can actually run at high-performing speeds and not just think you are.

Culture? I Already Have One, Thanks

"Not what it is, or what you want it to be; what does it need to be?"

WHAT IS A GOOD SALES CULTURE?

Passion. It's what separates the good from the great—the desire to spend the extra five minutes, to expect more than just the status quo, to create a process that generates unbelievable results.

Almost all of the managers I have talked to who said they had great sales cultures also said how passionate they and their people were about accomplishing the goals and objectives needed to succeed. There is a company out there that calls itself and the customer support it gives "fanatical," and its managers take this very seriously. If you talk to a salesperson in that company, you'll hear about how fanatical the person is about the company and her job.

But I have found some interesting common mistakes even in ProActive sales cultures.

When it comes to culture, the *first* sales-management mistake is to assume the company doesn't have one. Oh, your company has one alright. It may not be what you want or what you were expecting, but it has one.

183

The *second* mistake is to misunderstand the purpose of a sales culture. Here is what it is not: It is not a fancy phrase, a catchy slogan, or a document that is published so everyone can carry it around to prove the company has a culture. That's not the purpose of a sales culture.

A successful sales culture allows you to take advantage of rapidly developing changes, if appropriate, to influence a sales team's go-to-market approach. Culture cascades down from top management. It is executed at all ranks within and outside of the sales team. Great sales cultures morph. They change all the time so they can take advantage of what is in front of them and leverage the future.

So change the way you approach the customer. Change the way the customer wants to be treated. Adapt to new trends, new technologies, and more productive ways of doing things.

But remember, people hate to change. You hate to change. Typically, we do not like to change things up, especially if we know that what we are already doing is working.

You see the trends, the shifts in the market. You see what's happening. But are you determined to change what you are doing? That's a heck of a question. Change involves risk, and it involves something unknown. Sometimes it's better to continue what you're doing than to try the new stuff, sample it, set up an experiment—all the things you should do. But what about your culture? What about modifying it?

The brain likes a new idea like the body likes a plague.

This is a great phrase when applied to sales cultures. You need to adapt your culture to the trends and desires of the ever-changing market and customer demands.

It is natural to go through a process as you initiate change in the organization. Not to get sidetracked, but as you understand and modify your culture, remind yourself that you are going through a change process. The most famous definition of a change process is from psychologist Elisabeth Kubler-Ross:

The purpose of a sales culture is to change.

────────● KUBLER-ROSS'S STAGES ●────────

One of the most famous descriptions of the stages of grief was developed by Dr. Kubler-Ross in her book *On Death and Dying*. Dr. Kubler-Ross actually wrote about the stages that dying people tend to go through as they come to terms with the realization that they will soon be gone.

The same process has been borrowed by the business community to discuss change within an organization. Of course, not every organization going through change will experience all of these stages or experience them in this particular order. That said, let's look at the stages.

The first stage is denial. In this stage, organizations are unable or unwilling to accept that a loss has occurred or will shortly take place. This loss can show up as a change in the market, a change in buying habits, a new entry into the market, lack of growth, lack of returning customers, and the like. The "we have to work through it" and "we have to work harder" mentality exists. You hear people say, "It shouldn't be this hard."

When the realization occurs that a change is needed, people can feel as though they have fallen behind and they need to do something—anything. If they hurry up and do something, they may feel that things will return to normal. Typical actions are to increase selling price, add headcount, reorganize, or redistribute accounts.

After organizations have passed through denial and accepted that the loss has occurred (or will soon occur), they may begin to feel anger at the loss and the unfairness of it. They may become angry at the person or the situation that has been lost. Feelings of abandonment may also occur.

The next stage is bargaining. In this stage, people beg a "higher power" to undo the loss, saying things along the lines of, "I'll change if I can have this or that." This phase usually involves promises of better performance or making significant change to reverse the loss.

Once it becomes clear that anger and bargaining are not going to reverse the loss, organizations may sink into a depression stage where they confront the inevitability and reality of the loss and their own helplessness to change it. During this period, sales teams may experience top performers quitting or not performing at top speed. Salespeople may experience habit changes, or they may withdraw from activities while they process the loss. Lack of prospecting for new accounts, an unwillingness to give up old accounts, and apathy will set in. Salespeople and managers may also blame themselves for

Figure 20-1. The five stages of change.

causing or at least contributing to their loss, whether this is justified or not. Typically, they start throwing grenades and blaming everybody else.

Finally, if all goes according to plan, sales teams enter a stage of acceptance. They have processed their initial emotions, are able to accept that the loss has occurred and cannot be undone, and are once again able to plan for their futures and reengage in the next phase of the business cycle.

You can even see in Figures 20-1 and 20-2 that change involves behavior processes and time elements. If you want your culture to change, to adapt to the

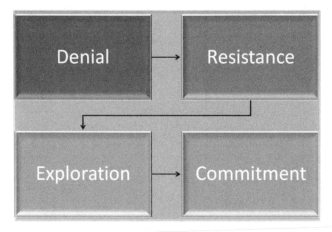

Figure 20-2. The sales-change process.

The Reorganization

The company was not doing really well. It had been doing the same thing for eight straight years, and although revenue was increasing, how the company got there was quite amusing.

It changed inventory methods, presold some equipment, and tried everything it could to keep up with revenue expectations. It even added 15 percent to the sales team at the end of the year to just "man the phones" and get revenue.

Something had to be done, so a new vice president of sales was brought on board. He knew of the change process and brought his management team together. "We need to change, and this is the process we are going to go through. The deal is I want to go through it in three months so we can get on with business."

In three months, the company laid off/terminated 25 percent of the sales team, got the rest of the team through the process, and hit its defining moment when the salespeople saw the commitments they were making could be accomplished (that is, they entered their acceptance stage).

The only reasons the company was able to get to where it wanted to go was the new vice president's commitment to change and the rest of the sales-management team's ability to see that it had to go through a process of change to get to the new culture.

"It's all about behavior and time," the VP said. "That's my job."

---

speed of the market, and to stay abreast of what is coming, managing your way through this process is key to managing cultures.

HOW DO YOU GET ONE?

Cultures are top down; change is bottom up. To start the change process, you need to define what you need to change—not where you want to go, but what you need to change. It is not important to know where you are going yet, but it is important to know whether you need to change something.

Once you have defined what needs to change, you have to define what you need to give up. Typically, what you need to give up is the way you are doing things now. It may have been good enough to get you to where you are today, but it may not be good enough to get you where you need to be. Examples could reside in how you go after major accounts, how you approach top accounts with a new product, whether you introduce an SFA system, or the way you handle sub-$20,000 accounts. Remember, you are not going to change the culture overnight. It's going to be one piece at a time—and how you implement change will determine your culture.

The culture-changing process looks something like Figure 20-3. As you go through the process of change, your behavior and your team's behavior will be key. Moreover, the time required to hit the objectives is under the manager's control. As a rule of thumb, the shorter amount of time to implement change, the better.

● HOW DO YOU KEEP IT ALIVE? ●

Once you have identified what needs to change and how you are going to know when the change has occurred, it's time to make sure you keep the change alive. Too often, sales management invests in a change, be it in sales training, sales automation, territory rules, or even sales compensation contests, that has very little effect after the initial announcement. The goals are to keep the change alive and to build off that change later on.

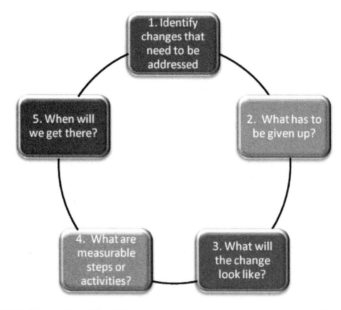

1. Identify changes that need to be addressed

2. What has to be given up?

3. What will the change look like?

4. What are measurable steps or activities?

5. When will we get there?

Figure 20-3. The culture-changing process.

The key to keeping change alive sits with the first-line managers. Here's a great story about that.

A sales team had just finished the year at 102 percent of quota. It was a struggle, and the team pulled out all the stops. The organization had just finished its fourth consecutive year of revenue growth, although this year was the smallest growth by percentage over quota and total dollars. The sales team was pleased with its results, but it just seemed too hard this year.

The sales VP knew he had to change some things around. Sales cycles seemed to be getting longer and average sales price (ASP) was staying flat. Something needed to change.

After two weeks of thinking about it (denial), he finally determined that the company's go-to-market strategy needed to change. This had been coming for a while, but he just did not want to start something and find out three months later that he was going down a wrong path. He talked to the CFO and the president, who were hesitant to change the way they were doing things (resistance). It had worked well over the past four years. Why mess with success? He got together with his key managers and some folks from finance and marketing, and they came to the conclusion (exploration) that they needed to change the way they sold.

They came up with a <u>three-tiered model</u>. Accounts under $5,000 per year would be handled by the customer service group. Accounts that were $5,000 to $20,000 would be handled by a new inside sales team. Prospects and customers over $20,000 would be handled by the outside field team. What this meant was that 40 percent of what the field team sold last year would be handled by customer service or the inside sales team. The risk was to grow the middle group without face-to-face sales calls and to get <u>the outside sales team prospecting for new business, which would be 30 percent of their quota</u>, as opposed to 10 percent the previous two years.

The first-line sales managers were convinced this was the right thing to do. They were able to persuade the sales team this was the right thing as well (commitment). The sales VP set a target of April 1 to have the new team assembled. First-line managers were told to get their teams assembled by the end of the first quarter. Some people left the company, even a pretty good first-line sales manager, and new ones joined. As a result, the team finished the year at 112 percent growth, set new records for new customers, saw new business at the midtier—and margins were never higher!

Here's what the company asked itself (and how it answered) during the sales change process.

1. **What needed to change?** *The way sales was getting the contracts. The face-to-face model, at the low end, was keeping the sales team from getting higher-dollar and higher-margin business.*

2. **What had to be given up?** *Sales under $20,000 were taken away from the field sales team. And this was how the field sales team had made its number for two consecutive years.*

3. **What will the change look like?** *The field sales team will have to get new business, a new inside sales team, and make customer service responsible for some revenue.*

4. **What steps or activities will be measured?** *A new team was in place by April 1. Successes for all teams are announced at an end-of-quarter celebration.*

5. **When will we get there?** *By April 1 for the organization and compensation plan; at the beginning of every quarter for quota obtainment. The field sales group will also be measured on prospecting and competitive takeaway wins.*

• PEOPLE LEAVE BOSSES •

> "People leave their immediate managers,
> not the companies they work for."
> —MARCUS BUCKINGHAM AND CURT COFFMAN,
> *FIRST, BREAK ALL THE RULES*

When implementing change, the golden rule is that the first-line manager has more influence over the employee than anyone else in the organization. The VP may be the greatest VP in the world, but if the salesperson's first-line manager is a dud and cannot implement the VP's change, then no amount of selling by the VP will influence the salesperson.

First-line managers need to be the best managers you have. Train them, keep them fresh, and keep them thinking. Support their ideas and let them make mistakes. If you are a first-line manager, do what I just mentioned. What have you done recently to make sure you have the best management team?

———————● TRAINING THE MANAGERS ●———————

I have been involved with training for over 20 years. I know that companies spend weeks training their sales teams and days or hours training sales managers to do their management jobs. Invest in your managers. Forty to sixty hours per year should be the minimum for training—that is, if you expect managers to manage, find leverage, and help make change a staple.

Oh, and all levels of management need training. You can tell how committed management is to change when you see sales training in action. It seems that any training not attended by sales managers and VPs ends up being less effective than when management sits through it.

There is a direct effect on success when the sales management team and the salespeople learn together. It creates a common vocabulary and a common bond. The new training sticks. This causes change, which modifies culture. You get the point. If managers are not all aware of what new skill sets the team is learning, it won't be long before the sales management team is under fire for not making its number.

Culture is a very important process managers are involved in all the time, from daily decisions to where the team needs to be in 6 to 12 months. It is up to you to be ahead of this curve, predict responses to change, and lead the team and the culture. Be ProActive. If you're not leading the change, get out of the way.

21

The More I Work,
the Better the Example

"Example management used to be the best way to show everyone
what you expect. Now, leadership takes a turn."

*I always wanted to be a good manager. Helping others. Making a team success-
ful. Helping a company to achieve its goals. I think I had the right reasons and
was promoted my third year to a district sales manager (DSM).*

*My first two years as a sales manager were great. My success was
measured by the team making its number, having the team finish second in
the nation my second year, weeding out the nonperformers, and hiring good
people.*

*The promotion to regional sales manager (RSM) came quickly, and I
thought I would have the same success as before. After all, everyone knew my
team worked hard and overperformed. We just had a swagger about us.*

*My first year as an RSM was not pretty. I took over a region that was well
below expectations. I had to work some people out of the organization, find new
ones, reenergize the team; heck, there was a lot to do. My goal was to finish the
year and set up success for year two. After all, it takes a while to turn a jumbo
jet around so it can fly right.*

Year two as an RSM was not going as planned. I had some key salespeople and a good sales manager leave. The salespeople were burned out, and the sales manager who left was the other candidate for the RSM job that I got. I expected him to find greener pastures, so it came as no surprise. But two months later when he took the top two salespeople who had worked for him over to his new company, well, that hurt. It was not a competitor, so we could not really stop them from going. I doubt it if we could have anyway.

Year two as an RSM finished up below plan, but better than year one. Yet with all the changes that happened, I considered myself lucky to finish where we did. Year three will be our year. The team is ready, all the distractions are gone, and we can focus on what we need to do to be successful.

After the first quarter of year three, my boss flew into town to observe the quarterly sales reviews. The pipeline looked good—not great, but good. It was a good session, and I was happy with the results. He then had a team meeting, without me, which is okay. I felt good about my team and if he wanted to know what was "really going on," that was his prerogative.

After a 90-minute sit-down with my team, he and I went to dinner. It was a very relaxed environment and during the conversation, he asked me a question: "What do you think is your best sales management strength?"

Without hesitation, I answered that I lead by example. I would never ask my team to do something that I wouldn't do myself. I was successful as a salesperson and as a sales manager. This RSM thing is bigger than I had thought, but I think I have it down.

"What are the top things you do that will cause you to be successful?"

I answered that I am involved in almost all major deals, I make sure the strategy for the big deals is solid, and I work with the salespeople on their pipelines. I lend my expertise without being overbearing. It is important that we have good margins on our deals and that we sell the right things. And I think my ability to go high into the C-suite helps the sales team enormously.

"Well," he said, "while you are doing that, who's running the region?"

"I am," I said.

"It seems like you are helping your sales team to sell, rather than managing it."

"I am doing what I know how to do, what I do best, what got me to where I am right now," I answered.

"What you are right now is a good sales mentor," he said. "You are not letting the salespeople sell. You are doing all the work. You have the most airline trips of any manager in the country. You know every deal intimately. While you

are busy selling, your team feels it cannot do anything without your permission. It's your way or the highway, and if you were not in on the close, the deal was not done correctly."

"You're kidding. I thought they liked me," I gasped.

"Oh they do. They just hate the way you impose your will on them. You seem to want to impart your wisdom and experience on them," he said.

"I have a lot of experience. What's wrong with that?" I asked.

"It's not your job."

"What is my job?" I wondered.

"Setting your team members up for success and letting them play the game. Your job is to make sure they have the correct game plan—that they have the best sales tools, the best opportunity to succeed. They have to succeed, not you. Your job is to have the faith, trust, and confidence that given the right tools, they will make the right choices. Your job is to figure out, in three to six months, which tools they will need to be successful. You have to live in the future and create a plan, a vision of what you want this team to be. Then you have to sell that vision every day, measuring the success and failures.

"You are so busy being supersalesperson, thinking you are doing the right thing, you really are the reason why this team is not successful. You have become the bottleneck that all decisions have to go through. You need to find out that by giving your top salespeople full control, you will ultimately have more control. You will also be doing your job.

"Think of yourself as an orchestra conductor. By the time you get out on stage, all the musicians are in place, the music is selected, and the order of the program is set. When it comes time to start, what are you going to do, go around and help each musician play his instrument? The conductor has to have the faith, trust, and confidence that when he lowers his baton, the musicians are going to play the right song, in the right key, at the right time."

"Okay, how do I learn how to be a conductor?" I asked.

"Now we are talking," he said.

WHILE YOU'RE BUSY BEING THE EXAMPLE, WHO'S STEERING THE SHIP?

Sales managers fall into this management trap all the time. They believe they need to *show* others how to be successful rather than *cause* others to be successful. The job of a great sales manager is to steer the ship, not sail the ship.

That's the crew's job, and because the crew members do it every day, they probably do it better than you, sorry to say.

Your job as a sales manager is to make sure the ship, and each individual crew member, stays on course. What they are doing is important. How they are doing it is not. That's for them to figure out, because everyone has a style of their own.

SETTING THE TACTICAL VISION

Your job is to set the vision of the team and measure what needs to get done to make that vision reality. Like a conductor, your job is to make sure everyone knows the songs. Your job is not to question everyone and ask if the instruments are in tune. That's the team's job. You have your job, the team members have theirs.

What's your job in setting the vision? There are three things you need to do.

1. Go six months into the future.

2. Create success.

3. Figure out what you did (and when you did it) over these last six months that got you to your vision.

> Figure out what the employee does well and encourage that, rather than try to put in something that isn't there.

Go Six Months into the Future

On a weekly basis, you need to set aside an hour or two and look into your crystal ball. What is happening all around you? What are your salespeople doing? What needs to be done? A good way to do this is play the numbers.

Divide up your sales team's activities into three categories. Pick three from the list here or make up three of your own. What three types of activities are the most important for your team to succeed?

- Prospecting
- Calling high
- Increasing ASP
- Forecasting
- Conducting executive presentations
- Doing demonstrations
- Conducting executive meetings with partners
- Conducting vendor meetings
- Conducting internal meetings
- Conducting broad and deep meetings

Now that you have the top three items, figure out what skill sets the team needs to focus on six months from now. What should the team be doing to be successful? Let's say you picked:

- Prospecting
- Increasing ASP
- Conducting broad and deep meetings

Now assign a percentage of how much time the team spends there today. For example:

- Prospecting—20 percent
- Increasing ASP—10 percent
- Conducting broad and deep meetings—10 percent

Next question: Six months from now, how much time should the team be spending on these items to be successful? For example:

- Prospecting—30 percent
- Increasing ASP—20 percent
- Conducting broad and deep meetings—30 percent

Now you have a tactical vision, a goal. Explain how you came up with these numbers, and then ask the team for a list of things that will happen

The Vision—Second Half—2009

	Today	Six Months	What Needs to Be Done
Prospecting	20%	30%	5 new calls per week per rep Updated database by end of month one 5 references per month per rep
Increasing ASP	10%	20%	Include consulting on every detail Offer product C on every deal Ask Marketing to use the product
Broad and Deep	10%	30%	Get 7 new division or additional companies per month per team Have sales manager visit 5 additional opportunities in major accounts per month

We need to accomplish these goals to take advantage of our new offering and help customers with their logistical problems.

Figure 21-1. An example of a tactical vision.

each month by team or individual in order to reach the new six-month goal. Figure 21-1 gives a good example.

Post your vision document where everyone can see the goals—and what must be done to achieve them.

This type of visioning is very different from strategic visioning. Strategic visioning is more about go-to-market issues; it requires major shifts in resources. Strategic visions are usually an annual event. Unless there are some major shifts in your market, it should stay a once-a-year item. Figure 21-2 shows the difference between short-term and long-term visions.

	Short-Term Vision	Long-Term Vision
Focus:	Objectives	Market demands
Time Frame:	Less than 6 months	12 months+
Reviewed:	Weekly	Quarterly
Measured:	Attainment of objectives	Reallocation of resources
Goal:	Support of long-term vision	Market opportunities

Figure 21-2. The differences between short-term and long-term visions.

-----------● **MEASURING THE VISION** ●-----------

Because your vision involves everyone, it should be noted that everyone ought to get involved in measuring it. This is why you post the goals and then get everyone involved in obtaining them. The secret here is to have the goals obtained and measured by teams.

When you do something with a partner, it seems like more gets done. So partner up your sales teams into natural groups—a group of two or a group of five, depending on what you want to accomplish. Measure the results in teams and not "who finished first." The goal again is to get everyone moving toward the vision, not to have a bell-curve result. Everyone has to win for the team to win.

Use the stoplight approach (see Figure 21-3). Start the team off at red, then yellow as it makes progress, then green when they accomplish the goal.

The Vision—Second Half—2009

Goal	Status	What Needs to Be Done
Teams	A B C D	
Prospecting	🚦🚦 🚦🚦	5 new calls per week per rep
	🚦🚦 🚦🚦	Updated database by end of month one
	🚦🚦 🚦🚦	5 references per month per rep
Increasing ASP	🚦🚦 🚦🚦	Include consulting on every deal
	🚦🚦 🚦🚦	Offer product C on every deal
	🚦🚦 🚦🚦	Ask marketing to use the product
Broad and Deep	🚦🚦 🚦🚦	Get 7 new division or additional companies per month per team
	🚦🚦 🚦🚦	Have sales manager visit 5 additional opportunities in major accounts per month

Red light = less than 25%
Yellow light= 80% accomplished
Green light = 100% accomplished

Figure 21-3. A chart that measures the vision using the stoplight approach.

If it gets to yellow and starts slipping, it goes back to red. Green means the team is on the goal. When all the lights are on, the goal has been accomplished. Update this chart every week or month. Keep it visible, and then when the team has completed the goal, check your culture and vision. Have they changed? Are they where you think they need to be?

● FOLLOW UP ●

Finally, keep in mind your job is to move the sales team toward the vision, not make sales; that's what you have the sales team for. It's hard to give up old habits. Selling comes naturally to you, and you must have sold well or you would not be in the position you are today.

As a manager or a senior manager, the goal is to make the revenue number. Too many sales managers want to take over sales calls, and too many managers want to sit in their ivory towers and direct a sales team but not make calls. The balance is part of the job, but in the end, it's about the company goals—and you're the one steering that ship. Here's to clear sailing ahead.

I'm the Manager, Right?

**"Managers believe authority and respect come
with the position. Employees, however,
will measure a manager differently."**

"I have been a manager for 12 years now: a first-line manager for six years,
then a second-line manager for five, and a vice president for one year. It seems
as though things are different now.

I want to say it feels like there is no below-the-radar anymore. Things are
very visible. I feel like I am under a microscope—not only to the sales team, but
obviously to the rest of the management team as well.

I also feel more reactive. The senior management team has agendas—and
it needs revenue to help meet those agenda items. While I am working hard to
help get everyone to their goals—whether they're about headcount, funding, or
finding more resources—I don't have time to be proactive about what my organization needs.

I'm the manager of the sales group; the leader of the sales team. If I just
keep my head down and stay focused, and make the number, it will all work
out. I am just very thankful I have a great team and a great boss."

That's trouble brewing.

PERSPECTIVE: I CARE ABOUT THE EMPLOYEES, BUT WHO CARES ABOUT ME?

That's a question that will get you into trouble. Your job is to maximize the portion of the company's revenue that you are in charge of—be it a sales region, a sales team, or worldwide sales responsibility—so the company can grow and prosper.

You also have a second job, and that would be to yourself and your loved ones. You owe it to them to get full market value for your services. If you consider yourself lucky to have a job, well that's good. But don't expect the company and the employees to take care of you when the new product is eight months late, your biggest customer goes to the competition, and your competitor takes two of your best salespeople. You can ride the luck wave when times are good, but when times are bad, all the arrows will be coming at you—and you'd better be ready.

Let's examine a field where top professionals get paid an outrageous amount of money to do something very simple. No, I am not talking about sales management; I am talking about professional sports.

A professional sports star makes quite a bit of money. In baseball, the figure is approaching $3 million per year, and in football, the number is around $1 million per year. OK, so good sales managers make a bit less than these folks, but a sports star's average earning time is less than five years. You could be in your sales-management career for about 20 years. The bottom line is that you will be making yourself and your company a lot of money over the next 20 years, but who is representing you?

Star athletes seem to go to the highest bidder. They know the shelf life for their services is very limited, so they try to maximize their potential. It was not always like this. Sports agents only became popular about 20–30 years ago. Before then, players played for the team that selected them, and "free agency" was nonexistent. The player played for a team, and the team paid him a "free market" wage. When team management decided he was through, it basically discarded him for someone younger and usually cheaper.

Now, when you work for a company and it is paying your wages and bonuses, you owe it to the company to give your 100 percent. By no means should you even think about undermining either your own reputation or the reputation of the one who signs your paycheck.

In other words, you have to take care of *you*. When you treat yourself as a businessperson, you will treat others the same way. When you look at what you do objectively, you will be able to see other things more objectively. How many times have you heard a sports star who just got traded from a first-place team to a mediocre team say something like, "Hey, when it comes down to it, it's a business"? It's that perspective that lets a person stay focused on the job; and it *is* a job. As fans, we think that athletes lead quite a life. The fame, glamour, attention, and money—they have it all. But they know it's a job. Outside of the top 10 percent, the rest are living for a paycheck. This is not to say you are not a superstar, but you may need to gain perspective on taking care of yourself.

To look at it from another perspective, when a sales manager puts too much focus on what he does, that is, when he thinks he is the center of it all, it hurts not only his reputation but the reputation of the sales team. The manager might say things such as:

- "Sales is the only group in this company that is giving 110 percent."

- "Without my sales team, you folks would not be where you are at today. You need to start coming up with some products that beat our competition for a change."

- "The sales organization here is world-class. We need to look at other parts of the company to figure out why we are not making goals."

Loss of perspective is obviously tied to too much of a single-minded approach. If you are too single-minded about your job, how do you think you are coming off to the employees and the company?

Once again, it would be very easy to misconstrue this as being all about you, with everyone else coming second. That is not what you should take away from this. The takeaway should be that when you have perspective—about you and the organization—you are a better employee and you will be better to all whom you serve.

COACHING THE WRONG WAY

When you look at sales as a business, you will find yourself coaching in a more positive way. Your personal frustrations can be compartmentalized and you can be more effective as a coach. The numbers are the numbers, but as a coach, you now know it is up to the salespeople—not you—to make their goals. Figure 22-1 summarizes this idea.

	"My Team" Centric	Business Centric
Problems	Ours	Employees
Rewards	Ours	Ours/Employees
Quota Obtainment	Ours	Ours/Employees
Compensation	Ours	Ours/Employees
Achievements	Ours	Ours/Employees
Glass Ceilings	Ours	Employees
Paradigms	Ours	Employees

Figure 22-1. Coaching perspectives.

So by gaining perspective, you can maximize the positives in a coaching environment and allow employees to accept responsibility for why they cannot do something or for why they hold themselves back.

Why is this an important topic? It's important because too many managers are blinded by their perspectives. In the worst cases, they are let go from organizations where they thought they were doing so well. The companies they work for may have just been bought and the new teams want none of the old teams. Or their companies buy other companies, move their headquarters, and do not retain employees who are not already at the new home office. There are many reasons why. So what can you do?

Take some time for yourself—strategy time. Personal time. Call it perspective-gaining time. The managers I talked to had numerous suggestions in this area. Here are their top five:

1. *Take a coffee break.* "Once a week I stop in at a coffee place on my way to work. I get a large coffee, call some friends, and check in. I sometimes meet with a customer, a headhunter friend, or a mentor. Once a month I'll meet with two other friends of mine who are VPs of sales in totally different industries, and we'll compare best

practices. It's a lonely job as VP of sales, and just to hear someone else going through what I am going through is helpful."

2. *Go to a training class.* "It's not just the training, but the attendees in the class are great. After the class, we'll get together and compare notes, swap issues, and really get a chance to gain some insight that I just never see when I am too close to an issue. I took a class two years ago and still regularly talk to about four people from that class. It's time for a new one."

3. *Set up a home office.* "The best thing I did was set up a remote office in my home. What's great about that is I do not have my files with me, so I cannot work on the usual day-to-day stuff. I just schedule my Blackberry for an 8:00–10:00 meeting that day, stay home, and get some great stuff done. I'll research a project, spend time looking at job boards for great candidates, research the industry and competitive issues, or even catch up on the *Wall Street Journal*. It's a great way to let the day-to-day stuff lay low for a while. Sometimes, I don't even get in until noon."

4. *Maintain a monthly goal sheet.* "Once a month I sit down with my goals for the month. I have two business and two personal ones. Every Sunday night, I make sure these goals are going to get some attention. It's not really important that I meet each goal every month, but as long as I am moving closer to the goal every week, making some progress, that's big in itself."

5. *Get involved in the community.* "I actually got involved with the city where I live. After getting involved in some small local stuff, I am now the mayor. Oh, it's a small town, and there are time constraints to say the least, but I really enjoy helping the community, and the contacts have been phenomenal. I am meeting people I never would have been able to meet in my job."

BEST PRACTICES: IT'S UP TO THEM

One of the best trade secrets managers shared with me is getting employees involved in employee-satisfaction surveys, 360-degree job interviews, and the

---

Best Practices: Not My Idea

"I took over a territory with quite a bit of turnover and low morale. I was seen as someone who did not know the industry and probably could not make a difference.

There were two ways of handling this. I could dictate what I wanted to get done, or I could enlist the help of the sales team.

I got the team members together and told them we needed to leverage their experience. I created a 'Best Practices Suggestion Box' and told them that for the next month, I would be collecting suggestions on what we should identify as our sales team's best practices. I only asked that they spend some time determining their own fates.

The first two weeks were quite slow, but then a great suggestion came in regarding how we do proposals. Essentially, we gave more influence to the salesperson in doing proposals, and everyone loved it. The employee was given a reward, and it made the list of our top five sales practices.

Within a month, we had our top five, and now once a quarter, we replace one with a new suggestion. The employees feel motivated, sales were never this good before, and I'm kind of like a hero executing their ideas. I must admit, I have put a few suggestions in the box myself, but most of the ideas came from the sales team, and even a few came from marketing. None have come from finance yet, but I'm working on it."

---

like. You will be amazed at the ideas that pour into an old-fashioned suggestion box. Keep one right outside your office, where salespeople or any employee can drop off a suggestion. You can get suggestions from remote locations by having a blind e-mail address where suggestions are handled by an administrator or someone from the human resources department. Make it an important topic in your monthly meetings so people feel involved and know they can be heard.

In sales, customers want to be heard. The funny thing is, so do employees, and by implementing their suggestions, employees feel empowered and involved. You will gain more respect from your team and your boss by implementing the team's ideas, not just your own.

---● **I WORK FOR . . .** ●---

It's a standard question, and it seems to generate so much discussion that it's worth mentioning. Answer the question: Whom do you work for?

A.   Myself

B.   The company

C.   My sales team

D.   The customer

E.   My family

F.   Some of the above

G.   All of the above

Think about it for a while and then circle your answer. Discussion on this could last hours, but in the final analysis, you work for the company. Sure, you work for all of the above, but the company provides your paycheck. That said, your company demands a learn-and-grow culture, or at least it *should*. What are you doing to keep your talents high? Are you sharpening your blade, keeping new ideas alive?

Look at this phrase: *Whatever got you where you are today is not good enough to get you where you need to be.*

This applies to you and your sales team. How you sell, how you go to market, and the skills required to do your job are different than they were just two years ago. You need perspective to stay ahead. Your company demands it. What are you doing every month to implement something different? The more time you spend gaining perspective, the more you will help your employer and everyone else on that answer list.

Authority is easy, respect is hard. Authority is given, respect earned. Getting others involved and putting yourself in a learn-and-grow situation are the best things you can do for yourself. You can earn respect by making the number, demanding it, or even hiring only people who think you can walk on water. The best sales managers have already tried these ideas and found that if they look at their positions, their customers, their sales teams, and their territories differently, that second right answer always shows up. They made the mistake of thinking they were supposed to come up with and implement ideas on their own.

The choice is yours.

EPILOGUE AND CALL TO ACTION

Seems like it's a lot to do. Sales management is a great opportunity to shape people's lives, be a success yourself, and represent your company to its customers.

Many things about management are critical: Hiring, corrective action, dashboards, metrics, and coaching are all tasks that must be mastered. If you had to come down to one critical area where most mistakes are centered, it would be speed.

Too fast is just as wrong as too slow. Too slow is death. If you go too fast, you miss the details. Speed kills.

With that said, there's a golden rule you may want to live by: Measure, measure, measure. It seems managers go too fast or too slow when they do not know what they want, what to expect from themselves, or what they should expect from their employees. Measurable weekly and monthly objectives—objectives that are outside of revenue—seem to be a key.

Change is good, even for change's sake. Make lemonade out of lemons. Go plant some lemon trees. Better yet, go build an orchard. The low-hanging fruit is there for you to take. Size it up, measure it . . . you'll get it.

INDEX

A players, *see* top performers
ability
  hiring based on, 174
  from training, 35–36
acceptance stage, 186
"account-based" territories, 123
Adams, Scott, 180
annual quota, 167
art, vs. creativity, 180
authority, vs. respect, 206

B and C players, as management focus,
  33–34
bad decisions, xvi
  and expenses, xv
bargaining stage, 185
behavior
  focus on, 41
  hiring based on, 174, 177
  motivating, 46–47
best practices, 204–205
boss
  asking about goals, 58
  as customer, 58
  sales manager as, 61–67
  staff leaving, 190
  see also managers
bottleneck, manager as, 194
buying process, 132–133
Buy/Sales process, example, 131

C players, *see* subpar performers
calendar, managing to, 69
calls, on upper management, 5
career-advancing decisions (CADs), 55
career-limiting decisions (CLDs), 55
Carnegie, Andrew, 77
Carville, James, 140
case study, on sales managers' role, 63–65
cell phones, and interruptions, 118
challenge, 80–81
  as motivator, 45–46
change, xvi–xvii, 184
  best time for, 119
  keeping it alive, 188–190
  in paradigms, 110–112
  realization of need, 185
  to sales meeting, 16–17
  in top performers, 26
change map, 101
change process
  definition, 184–187
  starting, 187–188
Chief Financial Officer (CFO), 165
CLDs (career-limiting decisions), 55
Clinton, Bill, 140
cloning, 176
coaching, 26, 108
  and leadership, 109–110
  timing for, 180
  wrong way for, 202–204